TUNISIA

MEDITERRANEAN CUISINE

TUNISIA

MEDITERRANEAN CUISINE

KÖNEMANN

Contents

List of Recipes

Level of Difficulty:

★   Easy
★★   Medium
★★★   Difficult

Hot & Cold Appetizers   8

Soups & Tagines   44

Couscous & Pasta   76

Fish & Seafood 106

Desserts & Pastries 154

Meat & Ragouts 128

Hot & Cold
Appetizers

Chakchouka

Preparation time: 30 minutes
Cooking time: 1 hour 25 minutes
Difficulty: ★★

Serves 4

2 cups/500 ml	live snails
1 or 2 sprigs	fresh thyme
1 or 2 sprigs	fresh rosemary
2 oz/50 g	garlic cloves
1 tsp	ground caraway seeds
½ tsp	ground coriander
14 oz/400 g	red squash

10½ oz/300 g	onions
4	moderately hot green chiles
7 oz/200 g	fresh tomatoes
¾ cup/200 ml	Tunisian olive oil
1 tbsp/17 g	tomato paste
1 tsp	North African harissa
½ tsp	chile powder
	salt and pepper

For the garnish:

parsley (optional)

Chakchouka with snails graces the tables of the Ksour Essef and Mahdia region in east Tunisia. The dish known as *chakchouka* is very popular across the whole of Tunisia. It's a vegetable ragout consisting of onions, fresh tomatoes, moderately hot green chiles, garlic, caraway seeds, tomato paste, harissa, salt, and pepper. The Mahdian cooks usually add green fava beans to the dish, while those of Ksour Essef supplement it with red squash. Some Tunisians also enrich it with potatoes, peas, or lentils.

Depending on the region and the cook, *chakchouka* can also be garnished with merguez (spicy sausage), octopus, shrimp, or eggs. Chokri Chteoui, a native of Ksour Essef, has an even more original approach and boldly adds snails to the dish. The children of this region take advantage of rainy days to go looking for the small gastropods in the forest, just as our chef did in his youth.

Our chef buys his live snails in the *souk* (the market). He keeps them and feeds them on semolina, thyme, and rosemary for several days, to give them a unique flavor before cooking them.

In his recipe, Chokri Chteoui has used two local varieties of snail: one is quite small with a white shell marked with a chocolate-colored spiral; the second, which resembles a snail from Burgundy, has a gray, finely-streaked shell. The "little grays" variety would also be perfectly suitable. If you use canned snails you won't need to cook them for as long as 45 minutes.

The squash used by our chef is an ordinary pumpkin, which is very easy to find. In Tunisian cookery, it's served with couscous, in *chakchouka*, and also is often reduced in soups for children's meals.

Rinse the snails thoroughly in several changes of water. Cook for 45 minutes in a pan of hot water, adding thyme and rosemary. Meanwhile, crush the garlic in a mortar with the caraway seeds, coriander, and salt and set aside.

Peel the squash and the onions and cut into large cubes. Cut the chiles into strips. Cut the tomatoes in two, deseed and quarter them and then cut into cubes.

Heat the olive oil in a saucepan. Add the onions to the hot oil and brown them, stirring all the while, to prevent them sticking to the bottom of the pan.

with Snails

Once the onions have started to brown, add the tomato paste, and mix gently. Add the fresh tomatoes, bring to the boil, keep it bubbling, and stir well. Season with salt and pepper.

Sprinkle the mixture with chile powder. Add the harissa, the cubes of squash, the chile, and the reserved garlic and spice mixture. Simmer for 15–20 minutes, until the vegetables are very tender. This mixture is the chakchouka.

As soon as the snails are cooked, drain them. Add them to the chakchouka. Reheat for about 10 minutes, stirring continuously. Serve hot, garnished with the parsley, if using.

Felfel Stuffed

Preparation time:	40 minutes
Cooking time:	15 minutes
Difficulty:	☆

Serves 4

1¼ lb/500 g	mild green chiles
8¾ oz/250 g	tomatoes
1	onion, chopped
3 tbsp/40 ml	olive oil
	oil for frying

For the stuffing

1¼ lb/500 g	whiting
1	potato

10 tbsp/150 g	chopped parsley
1	onion, chopped
	salt and pepper
1 slice	sandwich bread
4 tbsp/50 ml	olive oil
1 level tsp/5 g	ground coriander
1 tsp	cumin
3½ tbsp/50 g	harissa
1 level tsp/5 g	paprika
4	eggs

For the garnish:

	Chopped parsley

In Arabic, the word *felfel* means chiles. They are essential ingredients in Tunisian cuisine and feature in many recipes, bringing out the flavor of different dishes according to the spiciness of the chile.

Normally, Tunisian families use meat as a stuffing for *felfel*. But in the port of Bizerte, the stuffing is made of fish. This dish was originally prepared by fishermen's wives for their husbands to take to sea with them. Today, most families in Bizerte make this popular dish.

This regional specialty, which is well-known across the country, is enjoyed mainly in the summer. *Felfel* come from a plant belonging to the Solanaceous family (nightshade), like the tomato. They were introduced to North Africa by the Arab-Andalucians after their expulsion from the kingdom of Granada in Spain. The Tunisians grow many varieties of the plant and eat the chiles either fresh or dried.

Their spicy, or even red-hot flavor, comes from a substance called "capsine." Capsine makes you salivate and it helps to stimulate the digestion. Chiles are usually used for flavoring, but here they are used as vegetables. Our chef suggests that you peel them after you've fried them. That way, they retain their fresh green color and are easier to digest.

Whiting is an ideal fish to use for this stuffing. Its flesh, very delicate and white, separates easily into layers. Found on the market stalls in Bizerte, you can tell whether whiting is fresh by its red gills, bright eyes and metallic color. You can use sardines as an alternative to whiting. When you prepare the stuffing, you can also put a small quantity to one side to make *kefta*, which are small croquettes. They will be most welcome as part of a *kemia* (a collection of colorful small dishes) and much appreciated when you drink your aperitif!

With your thumb, gently push the chile stalk towards the inside of the pepper, then pull the stalk towards you to extract the seeds. Clean the stalks under running water to remove the seeds and place to one side.

Poach the whiting fillets for about 10 minutes in water with salt and pepper added. Chop the fish finely when cooked. Cook the potato in water and mash it.

Prepare the stuffing by mixing the chopped whiting and the potato in a bowl. Add the chopped parsley and onion.

with Fish

Crumble the sandwich bread slice and add it to the stuffing. Pour in 4 tbsp (50 ml) olive oil and mix together.

Season the stuffing with salt, pepper, coriander, cumin, harissa, and paprika. Add the eggs and mix. Prepare the sauce by peeling and seeding the tomatoes. Dice them finely. Brown them with the chopped onion in 3 tbsp (40 ml) of olive oil. Add salt and pepper. Set aside.

Using your fingers, stuff the chiles. Put the stalks back and then fry the stuffed chiles in oil for 2–3 minutes. Arrange on a plate on top of the tomato sauce. Garnish with chopped parsley.

Bissara

Preparation time:	*30 minutes*
Cooking time:	*30 minutes*
Difficulty:	☆

Serves 4

1	onion, chopped
2	garlic cloves, crushed
3½ tbsp/50 ml	olive oil
1 tbsp/17 g	tomato paste
2	tomatoes

4	eggs
1¼ lb/500 g	green fava beans
	(broad beans)
	salt and pepper

Tunisian hospitality is recognized all over the world. If you have the good fortune to be invited to share a meal with a family, you might be surprised to find that the appetizers follow one after another.

Bissara with green fava beans is generally offered as the second hot appetizer. It is a traditional peasant recipe. In this farming region, where women work on the land and look after the children, this specialty has the advantage of being nourishing and quick to prepare. Fava beans are an important ingredient in Tunisian dishes. Particularly rich in proteins and vitamins—even when dried—they are very nutritious. They belong to the same family as peas, which can be used instead of fava beans in this recipe.

Originating from Persia and Africa, fava beans have been known and eaten in the Mediterranean region since ancient times. They are both spring and summer vegetables, and are sometimes served cold in salads. When they're young, you don't need to remove their delicate skin.

Onions, which are an ingredient of *bissara*, are found in many Tunisian recipes. According to our chef, they help the body fight against the effects of the heat.

In this farming region, the people tend to live on what the farm produces: eggs, poultry, vegetables, fruit, and so on, so it's no surprise to find a soft-boiled egg as the accompaniment to *bissara*. Eggs have been eaten for their nutritional value and versatility since ancient times. They will keep for a minimum of three weeks in the least cold part of the fridge. Store them pointed end down, and never wash the shells; otherwise the eggs will absorb strong odors.

Although *Bissara* is a traditional appetizer from the Béja region, you can serve it as a main dish.

Brown the chopped onion in 3½ tbsp (50 ml) of olive oil for 3–4 minutes. Add the crushed garlic to the onion. Mix well.

Add the tomato paste to the onion and garlic, and mix well.

Peel the tomatoes and deseed them. Cut them into small cubes and add to the mixture. Season with salt and pepper. Cook for approximately 5 minutes.

Stir and add 7 tbsp (100 ml) water.

After shelling the fava beans and removing the skins, add them to the mixture. Cook for 15–20 minutes.

Break the eggs into a ramekin. Then transfer them to the mixture, cover and poach for approximately 8 minutes. Using a skimming ladle, remove. Arrange with the fava beans and the tomato sauce on plates.

Ojja

Preparation time:	35 minutes
Cooking time:	40 minutes
Difficulty:	✶

Serves 4

5 tsp/25 g	tomato paste
3¹/₂ tbsp/50 ml	olive oil
2	garlic cloves, crushed
5 oz/150 g	tomatoes
1 tsp	caraway seeds
3¹/₂ oz/100 g	mild green chiles, deseeded and diced
4	eggs

For the meatballs:

5 oz/150 g	ground beef
1	onion, finely diced
5 tsp/25 g	chopped parsley
1 tsp	caraway seeds
1 level tsp/5 g	dried mint
1 tsp	harissa
	salt and pepper

For the garnish:

	parsley (optional)

Although *ojja* is a very popular specialty of Nabeul, it's also a great favorite in the Tunis region. This recipe, made from tomatoes, mild green chiles, and eggs, can be supplemented with lamb's brains, dried herrings, merguez, shrimp or even meatballs, according to a family's taste.

Very easy to make, *ojja* is generally served as the second appetizer or the main dish. According to our chef, this dish is particularly popular with young couples. "It's quick to prepare and ideal for anyone who works."

The meatballs that accompany this dish can be made with ground lamb or ground beef. Mohamed Boujelben suggests that you oil your hands lightly to prevent the mixture from sticking.

Meatballs are found in many Tunisian dishes, and are delicious. Chopped flat-leaf parsley gives them their delicate

flavor and their specific aroma. This herb, which is available all year round in the markets, must be very green and fresh, with stiff leaves and stalks.

Each herb and spice gives the meatballs their particular character. Dried mint, another of the ingredients, is also very widely used in oriental and Tunisian cuisines. This aromatic, fragrant plant is distinguished by its oblong or oval leaves. With caraway, it is the oblong, brown seeds that are used as a spice. It has a slightly sharp, hot flavor. Simmering in a dish brings out its aroma.

Although *ojja* varies according to a family's taste, it must always include eggs. Our chef suggests that you adjust the seasoning by adding a pinch of salt to the yolks.

This traditional dish, which deserves to be more widely discovered, is currently very fashionable in Tunis.

Prepare the meatball mixture, by putting the ground beef, finely diced onion, chopped parsley, caraway seeds, dried mint, and harissa into a bowl. Add salt and pepper. Mix well together.

Take a little of the mixture between your hands and roll it into small balls.

Heat 3¹/₂ tbsp (50 ml) of olive oil in a pan. Add the tomato paste and mix. Add the crushed garlic and diced tomatoes. Season with salt and pepper. Add 1 tsp of caraway seeds, and mix. Fry gently for approximately 5 minutes.

with Meatballs

Add some hot water to the mixture. Cook for approximately 20 minutes. Add the diced chiles. Cook for approximately 10 minutes.

Add the meatballs. Cook for approximately another 7 minutes.

Break the eggs into a bowl, then place them carefully on top of the mixture in the pan. As soon as the whites have set, arrange on a serving dish. Garnish with parsley, if using.

Ojja with Shrimp

Preparation time:	15 minutes
Cooking time:	15 minutes
Difficulty:	✫

Serves 4

1¼ lb/500 g	mild green chiles
8¾ oz/250 g	tomatoes
2	garlic cloves, crushed
7 tbsp/100 ml	olive oil
2 tbsp/35 g	tomato paste
1 tsp	harissa
1¼ lb/500 g	small shelled shrimp

1 tsp	ground cumin
4	eggs
	salt and pepper

For the garnish:

| | ground cumin |

Ojja is a traditional Tunisian specialty. It is a hot appetizer that is similar to the Basque *piperade* with its basic ingredients of tomatoes, mild green chiles, and eggs. The dish comes from Nabeul, the pottery capital, in the Cap Bon region, and is prepared in a variety of ways. According to each family's preference, *ojja* can include lamb's brain, dried herring, or merguez. *Ojja* with scrambled eggs and harissa is nicknamed *kadhaba*, which means "untruthful woman!"

For his part, our chef wanted to add a touch of sophistication by making this recipe with small pink shrimp. These crustaceans, highly prized for the delicacy of their flesh, are often sold in their shells. They impart the taste of the sea to this hot appetizer. If you buy pre-cooked shrimp, add them to the mixture at the same time as the chiles.

Tomatoes are closely associated with Tunisian culinary heritage. They must be firm, plump, shiny, and preferably have a uniform color. If the tomatoes are very juicy, there's no need to add the half glass of water.

It's vital to add the ground cumin at the last moment to avoid a bitter flavor. This aromatic plant, which has its origins in Turkestan and has been spreading across the Mediterranean region for centuries, is distinguished by its hot, spicy, and slightly sharp taste. Follow the example of our chef and use it as decoration for your plates too. Its slightly ocher color harmonizes perfectly with the hot colors of the *ojja*.

This simple appetizer is easy to prepare and is quite filling. If you haven't tried it before, it's high time you discovered it.

Cut the chiles into thick slices and the tomatoes into cubes.

Brown the garlic with 7 tbsp (100 ml) olive oil in a saucepan. Add the cubed tomatoes and simmer for approximately 3 minutes.

Add the tomato paste and the harissa. Simmer for approximately 3 minutes.

from Nabeul

Add the shelled shrimp. Pour in ½ glass of water and reduce for approximately 2 minutes.

Add the sliced chiles. As soon as the sauce becomes smooth and the chiles have softened, add salt and pepper, and sprinkle the ground cumin into the mixture.

Break the eggs into a bowl and beat to an omelet mix. Stir them into the mixture. Cover the pan and cook them over a low heat for approximately 3 minutes. Arrange on a plate and garnish with a touch of cumin.

Stuffed Small Vegetables,

Preparation time: 55 minutes
Cooking time: 40 minutes
Difficulty: ★★

Serves 4

4	tomatoes
2	lemons
10¹/₂ oz/300 g	zucchini
8³/₄ oz/250 g	eggplants
7 oz/200 g	mild green chiles
1¹/₄ lb/500 g	potatoes
	salt and pepper

For the stuffing:

¹/₄ cup/50 g	rice
1¹/₄ lb/500 g	ground beef
1	onion, chopped
6¹/₂ tbsp/100 g	chopped parsley

6¹/₂ tbsp/100 g	grated Swiss cheese
1 tsp	caraway seeds
1	egg, beaten
1 tsp	harissa
	cooking oil

For the tomato sauce:

1³/₄ lb/750 g	tomatoes
2	garlic cloves, crushed
7 tbsp/100 ml	olive oil
1 pinch	saffron strands, in ¹/₂ glass water

For the garnish:

	chopped parsley

Known as *doulma*, this mixture of stuffed small vegetables from the Tunis area is typical of the Mediterranean region as a whole. Consisting of zucchini, eggplants, tomatoes, mild green chiles, potatoes, and lemons, this refreshing dish is mainly served in summer.

According to a family's taste, the stuffing is prepared with ground beef or ground lamb. The highly flavored meat goes perfectly with the vegetables. When you fry the vegetables, our chef recommends that you lightly brush the stuffing with beaten egg and all-purpose flour. This way, they'll retain their attractive appearance.

It's best to start by frying the potatoes. These vegetables, originating from Latin America, are eaten throughout the world. Select the hardest potatoes with a smooth skin, unblemished and without any sprouts. They keep perfectly well in a dry, cool place, preferably out of direct light. On contact with the air, the inside of a potato tends to go black. Leave peeled potatoes immersed in cold water while waiting to use them.

The zucchini and eggplants must be added at the same time. These summer vegetables are a great favorite of Mediterranean people. Preferably choose the smaller, tastier vegetables for this recipe. With their strong flavor, eggplants go extremely well with the tomato sauce. They must be unblemished, with a smooth, intact, and firm skin. As for the zucchini, you can judge their freshness by how uniform their color is. They are not usually peeled, but you need to scrape the skins.

In the Tunis region, stuffed small vegetables are often enjoyed as a family meal. According to your preference you can either pour the tomato sauce straight onto the vegetables or serve it separately.

Prepare the stuffing by boiling the rice for about 10 minutes. Mix the ground beef, chopped onion, chopped parsley, grated Swiss cheese, and boiled rice in a bowl. Add the salt, caraway seeds, and harissa. Mix well. Allow to stand for approximately 10 minutes.

For the sauce, wash, peel, and deseed the tomatoes; then reduce them to a purée. Wash the remaining tomatoes and the lemons, zucchini, eggplants, and chiles. Peel the potatoes. Cut the zucchini into chunks. Deseed the chiles. Scoop out all the vegetables.

Prepare the sauce by browning the prepared purée and crushed garlic cloves in 7 tbsp (100 ml) olive oil. Add salt and pepper. Add the saffron water. Fry gently until the vegetable water has evaporated. Add a little extra water and cook for approximately 10 minutes.

Tunis-Style

Blanch the scooped out lemons. Fill the zucchini, potatoes, tomatoes, lemons, and chiles with the stuffing.

Heat the cooking oil. Brush the vegetable stuffing with a little beaten egg. Carefully immerse the vegetables in the hot oil.

Place the stuffed vegetables on a dish. Pour the sauce over the top. Bake in the oven at 350 °F/180 °C for 10 minutes. Arrange the small vegetable parcels on a serving dish. Garnish with a little chopped parsley.

Radhkha

Preparation time: 40 minutes
Difficulty: ★

Serves 4

1³/₄ lb/800 g	tomatoes
5 oz/150 g	mild green chiles
2¹/₂ oz/70 g	tuna in oil
4	garlic cloves
7 tbsp/100 ml	olive oil
¹/₂	a lemon
	salt

For the garnish:
6¹/₂ tbsp/100 g   black olives

When the heat rises above 104 °F/40 °C, the inhabitants of Tozeur eat *radhkha* to cool themselves down. Tunisian women make small crepes of fine semolina, salt, and water, called *rougag*, as an accompaniment to this salad.

The preparation of the *radhkha* is typically Mediterranean. All the ingredients—garlic, tomatoes, mild green chiles, and tuna—are crushed in a mortar with a pestle called a *mihras* in Tunisian. The use of this round container, which varies in size, goes back to ancient times. Whether they're made of olive wood, thick china, marble, or stone, the pestle and mortar have proved to be essential tools in the creation of many North African, Southern European, and Far Eastern dishes.

Garlic brings its own distinctive flavor to this appetizer. Grown for over 5,000 years, this bulb has the reputation of promoting good health. In spring, the new garlic appears in the markets. It's fairly gentle in flavor and easy to peel. Select very hard, plump cloves. Keep them in the fridge in the crisper. However, the ordinary garlic that is available throughout the year must be stored in a dry place. If it gets damp, it tends to sprout.

Chiles, like tomatoes, are essential ingredients of the Tunisian culinary tradition. Discovered in the New World by Christopher Columbus, these plants were introduced into the Tozeur region by the Arab-Andalucians. There are a huge number of varieties of fresh and dried chiles in Tunisia. Their spicy flavor ranges from mild to very strong. To make this recipe, you need to deseed and dice them finely before grinding them up. Remember to rinse your hands after handling them.

Radhkha is a salad with quite a spicy taste and its colorful appearance is most attractive.

Wash the tomatoes and dice them.

Wash the chiles and split them in two. Deseed and dice them. Flake the tuna.

Peel the garlic cloves. Grind them in a mortar.

from Tozeur

Put the diced tomatoes and chiles in a bowl, and grind with a pestle. Add the ground garlic cloves.

Pour 7 tbsp (100 ml) of olive oil into the bowl and add the flaked tuna. Mix. Crush the mixture with the back of a large spoon.

Add the salt and squeeze the half a lemon into the mixture, removing any pits that fall in. Arrange the radhkha salad on plates. Garnish with black olives.

Fava Bean Salad

Preparation time:	10 minutes
Cooking time:	15 minutes
Difficulty:	★

Serves 4

4 lb/2 kg	fresh fava beans (broad beans)
1	lemon
2 tsp	harissa
²/₃ cup/150 ml	olive oil

2 tsp	cumin
	salt
½ tsp	pepper

Fava bean salad with cumin and harissa is a great favorite with Tunisian families. Locally, it's known as *m'dammes* and is dead easy to make. The fava beans, called *foul* in Tunisian, are grown all over the country. To enjoy them at their best, Mohamed Bouagga recommends preparing this dish with young beans.

The way to recognize older beans is that they have a black thread running around the pod. Young beans have a tender green thread. When you use young beans, there is no need to remove their skin as it's relatively thin, but older beans are better with their skins removed. This is an easy task when the beans are cooked. To keep their fresh green color, Mohamed Bouagga adds lemon to the cooking water, using the rind of the lemon used in the recipe.

Originally, *m'dammes* was served hot, and the cooking liquid was retained. It goes with the traditional tomato sauce with harissa and cumin. If you want to bring out the garlic flavor, add two chopped garlic cloves to this salad.

Many westerners aren't used to eating highly seasoned or very spicy dishes. To get used to the strong flavor we recommend that you add the harissa bit by bit. Taste the dish at each stage of its preparation to gauge its strength, rather than adding the two teaspoons of harissa straightaway.

If you want to make your own harissa, it is very easy. Simply crush 1 lb (450 g) *felfel* (small dry red chiles), having deseeded and softened them in cold water. Next grind them in a mortar. Add 4 garlic cloves reduced to a paste and season with two pinches of caraway seed and two pinches of coriander. Finally, add salt to the mixture and put the harissa paste into a container, covering it with olive oil to keep it fresh. Then you can use and abuse it, as most Tunisians like to do.

Shell the fava beans and wash them, but don't remove the skins. Squeeze the lemon and put the juice to one side.

Put the lemon rind into the cooking water, and bring to the boil.

Cook the fava beans in the lemon water for 10–15 minutes. When they begin to wrinkle, they're cooked.

with Cumin and Harissa

Drain the fava beans. First, leave them to cool at room temperature. Then put them in a cool place. Discard the lemon rind.

Prepare the seasoning by putting the harissa and olive oil into a bowl. Add the cumin and the reserved lemon juice. Season with salt and pepper.

Season the fava beans with the harissa, cumin, and olive oil sauce (add it bit by bit, tasting, to control how spicy you want it). Serve chilled.

Tunisian

Preparation time: 25 minutes
Cooking time: 45 minutes
Difficulty: ★

Serves 4

2¼ lb/1 kg	octopus
½	lemon
5 oz/150 g	fresh tomatoes
1	small onion
3½ tbsp/50 g	chopped flat-leaf parsley
3½ tbsp/50 ml	olive oil
1	lettuce
	salt and pepper

For the garnish:

2 oz/50 g	radish
16	black olives
2	lemons, optional

Octopus salad is a culinary delight from Mahdia, one of the most important ports in Tunisia. These marine animals, also called octopods, have horny mouths and eight tentacles with suckers. The fishermen of Mahdia usually bring back medium-sized fish weighing between 1¾ lb (800 g) and 3lb (1.5 kg). They are not allowed to capture the smallest specimens, and large octopuses have fairly tough flesh and are less sought after.

To catch them, fishermen use containers derived from amphorae known as gargoulettes. The gargoulettes are left in the sea in the evening, and octopuses adopt them as hiding places. Then all the fishermen need to do the next morning is to hoist the lot onto their boats.

The time for the best Tunisian octopus is between September and December. For the rest of the year, salads are made from octopus dried in the sun on nets hanging from walls. Preserved this way, it can be kept for several months, but it then needs to be rehydrated the night before cooking. Our salad can also be prepared with calamari or cuttlefish.

Octopus must always be tenderized at least 15 minutes before you start cooking it. In Tunisia, cooks either hit the fish a number of times against a wall, or lay it on a board and beat it forcefully with a stick. To check you have tenderized it enough, gently pull the skin at the level of a sucker. It should tear slightly.

When you start cooking the octopus, the flesh and the water you poach it in turn crimson. Do not cook it for more than 45 minutes, as it can become rubbery. Use the point of a knife to prick it to see if it's tender and cooked. When it is ready, remove the octopus from the liquid and plunge it in a container of iced water to prevent further cooking.

Rinse the octopus and cut it into large pieces. Tenderize it by beating it a number of times with a meat mallet or a stick.

Immerse the octopus in a stockpot of cold water. Bring it gently to the boil and cook for approximately 45 minutes, until tender.

Using a slotted spoon, remove the octopus pieces from the cooking juice. Transfer to a saucepan filled with iced water.

Octopus Salad

Meanwhile, squeeze the lemon, placing the juice to one side. Chop the tomatoes. Peel and chop the onion.

Cut the octopus into small strips. Mix the tomatoes, onion, and parsley in a bowl. Add the octopus strips to this salad.

Drizzle the lemon juice and a little olive oil over the salad. Season with salt and pepper. Arrange it on a bed of lettuce leaves. Garnish the salad with black olives, small pieces of radish, and slices of lemon, if using.

Ganaria

Preparation time: 40 minutes
Cooking time: 25 minutes
Difficulty: ★★

Serves 4

3	lemons
6	large artichokes
2	eggs

For the filling:

1	crystallized lemon
3½ oz/100 g	mozzarella
3½ tbsp/50 g	pitted green olives
2 medium-sized	tomatoes
3½ tbsp/50 g	parsley

3 tsp/10 g	capers
1 tsp	harissa
7 tbsp/100 ml	olive oil
	salt and pepper

For the garnish:

	lettuce leaves (optional)

Ganaria salad is a refreshing mixture based on artichokes. A great favorite of the people of Tunis and Nabeul, this cold appetizer is popular in the spring.

Scooping out the artichokes is the tricky part of this recipe. Originating from Sicily, artichokes are hardy plants that belong to the Compositae family. They are often used in Mediterranean cooking. The fleshy, tender heart of the artichoke is served after its choke has been removed. The base of the leaves is also edible. Select large artichokes for this recipe, as they're easier to fill. Avoid artichokes with leaves that have lost their fresh green color. If you want to keep them for a few days, keep their stems in water. After preparing them, they must be kept in water with lemon juice added until they are needed, to stop them going brown.

All the filling ingredients are typically Mediterranean. A prime example is *mozzarella*, an Italian cheese with a sweet, slightly tangy, flavor, made in the Latium and Campanula regions from buffalo milk. *Mozzarella* is bought in a number of forms, usually preserved in salted water, and when cooked it forms a stringy paste with a barely discernible crust.

This sunshine salad uses capers as a condiment. Capers are the flower bud from the caper shrub, a small tree growing wild in Tunisia, and they are found in many regional dishes. Our chef recommends that you select very small capers, which are valued for their delicate flavor and pronounced scent.

As for harissa, its reputation goes far beyond the boundaries of Tunisia. Harissa is renowned for enlivening a large number of dishes. Harissa is still homemade in some families—a paste made from dried, chopped, red chiles, seasoned with salt, garlic, caraway seeds, and olive oil.

In a bowl, squeeze the juice of 2 lemons and add a little water. With a sharp knife, remove the stem, and peel the 6 artichokes by scooping them out right down to the heart. Remove the choke with a spoon. Put the artichoke hearts in the lemon water.

Take 2 artichoke hearts and slice into ¼ in (2–3 mm) thin strips and put in the lemon water. Put the 4 remaining hearts in boiling water and cook for approximately 25 minutes. Hard-boil the eggs and shell them.

Prepare the ingredients for the filling by thoroughly peeling the crystallized fruit. Finely dice the skin, the mozzarella, and green olives.

Salad

Chop the parsley very finely; finely dice the tomatoes and hard-boiled eggs.

Put all the filling ingredients into a bowl. Add the artichoke strips and the capers. Mix gently. Squeeze the juice of the remaining lemon into the mixture and stir. Season with salt, pepper, harissa, and the olive oil. Stir together.

Drain the cooked artichoke hearts. Fill them with the ingredients. Arrange the ganaria salad on the plate. Garnish with lettuce, if used and decorate the plates with a trickle of olive oil, flavored with harissa.

Mechouia

Preparation time: 20 minutes
Cooking time: 15 minutes
Difficulty: ★

Serves 4

4¹/₂ lb/2 kg	mild green chiles
1¹/₄ lb/500 g	tomatoes
3	garlic cloves, finely chopped
7 tbsp (100 ml)	olive oil
1 tsp	caraway seeds
4	eggs

1 can	tuna in oil
5 tsp/25 g	pitted black olives, thinly sliced
5 tsp/25 g	pitted green olives, thinly sliced
	salt

For the garnish:

paprika (optional)
olive oil (optional)

In Arabic, *mechouia* means "broiled." This Tunisian salad, which is typical of the Cap Bon region and the rest of the country, is another legacy of the Arab-Andalucian culinary tradition. Settling in Tunisia after the fall of the kingdom of Granada in 1492, the Andalucians brought the tomato, chile, and bell pepper with them. According to our chef, the discovery of these plants "revolutionized" traditional recipes: "Before the arrival of the Arab-Andalucians, Tunisian cuisine was essentially based on the color yellow. From that time onwards, it altered, turning red."

Today, the splendid Cap Bon region, renowned for its market garden produce, offers its inhabitants all the necessary ingredients to make this delicious appetizer. In some families, the flavor of the tomatoes dominates the *mechouia*. Other families prefer to use very few tomatoes or even completely omit them from the mixture. However,

mild green chiles, *felfel*, are an essential ingredient. If you want a spicier flavor, don't remove their seeds.

Traditionally the vegetables in this salad are broiled on the *kanoun*, a brazier. The aroma of the charcoal permeates the mixture, giving it an inimitable flavor. But for Rafik Tlatli, the success of this recipe is based on the way you crush the chiles, which should be done using a pestle and mortar.

Tunisians are very fond of tuna. Catching these migratory fish is an important economic resource for the country. Sold in cans, Tunisian tuna in oil is known throughout the world. Drain and flake the tuna before serving.

Mechouia salad is mainly served in summer, when tomatoes and chiles are to be found in the markets, and is very refreshing.

Broil the chiles and tomatoes on an aluminum sheet at 400 °F/200 °C for 10 minutes. Drain the tomatoes in a colander. Carefully peel the skin from the chiles using your fingers.

Split the chiles in half lengthwise and deseed them.

Peel and deseed the tomatoes. Chop the chiles. Crush the tomatoes and chiles in a bowl, using a pestle.

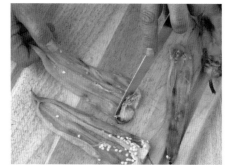

Salad

Add the garlic to the tomato and chile mixture.

Season the mechouia *salad* with the olive oil, caraway seeds, and salt. Mix well. Cook the eggs in salted water for approximately 12 minutes. Shell and slice them.

Using 2 spoons, make salad quenelles. Arrange them on the plate and add the flaked tuna, the thinly sliced green and black olives, and the egg slices. Sprinkle with paprika, if using. Add a trickle of olive oil, if using.

Mosaic Salad

Preparation time:	20 minutes
Cooking time:	25 minutes
Difficulty:	★

Serves 4 to 6

2	potatoes
2	carrots
2	red beets
¾ cup/100 g	peas
3½ oz/100 g	navy beans
2	eggs
2	onions

½	bunch flat-leaf parsley
7 tbsp/100 ml	Tunisian olive oil
1	lettuce
1 can	sardines in Tunisian olive oil
6½ tbsp/100 g	black or green olives
	salt and pepper

Mosaic salad from Sfax is a favorite springtime treat in Tunisia. At this time of the year, the markets are full of small, tender, colorful, and tasty vegetables. The spring carrots are juicy and fragrant, and there is a wide variety of vegetables to choose from. As the fancy takes them, gourmets add artichokes and turnips to their salad as well as the seafood.

As prolific producers of sun-ripened fruits and vegetables, Tunisians usually prepare salads according to the season: early produce in spring; tomatoes, onions, and cucumbers in summer. Once the season has finished, the surplus vegetable harvest is dried in the sun and stored for the winter.

Potato cultivation is a fast-expanding industry in Tunisia, and it takes place throughout the year. New potatoes appear from March to May, the height of the season is between June and October, and the end of the season is from November to February.

Olives reach maturity at the beginning of November. Initially green, they turn black when they are very ripe, at which point they are squeezed to produce the highly renowned Tunisian olive oil. In this recipe, green and black olives are equally suitable.

What could be more natural than to add sardines in oil to a salad from Sfax? The ports of Sfax, Mahdia, and Kelibia have long been known for their sardine fishing. Several varieties of sardines are sold in cans, either in vegetable or olive oil, tomato sauce, or sometimes even flavored with harissa. Some families preserve sardines themselves: removing the heads, gutting and cleaning them, the sardines are then dipped in very hot oil and preserved in a hermetically sealed jar of olive oil.

Peel the potatoes, carrots, and the red beets. Cut into small cubes. Shell the peas. Cut the navy beans into 1 in (2 cm) lengths. Cook everything separately in boiling water "al dente" (until they're just cooked), or until softer, according to taste.

As soon as they're cooked, use a slotted spoon to transfer the navy beans and peas into a basin of ice water to keep their fresh green color.

Hard-boil the eggs for 10 minutes in boiling water, peel them, and cut into quarters. Peel the onions. Chop the onions and parsley finely.

from Sfax

Mix the potatoes, carrots, peas, onions, navy beans, and parsley in a dish to make a salad.

Season the salad with a trickle of olive oil, salt, and pepper. Separate the lettuce leaves, rinse, and spin them. Open the can of sardines and drain them.

Make a bed of lettuce in your serving dish. Arrange the vegetable salad on top. Garnish with cubes of red beet, egg quarters, and olives. Arrange the sardines on the salad. Serve chilled.

Fethi Tounsi's

Preparation time:	20 minutes
Cooking time:	10 minutes
Difficulty:	✮

Serves 4

7 oz/200 g	fresh green chiles
3½ oz/100 g	fresh red chiles
2	tomatoes
⅔ cup /150 ml	olive oil
1 tsp	ground coriander

1 tsp	cumin
2	garlic cloves
4	herring fillets
4 tsp/20 g	capers
	salt and pepper

For the garnish (optional):

3½ tbsp/50 g	pitted black olives
	mint leaves

In Arabic, *renga* means herrings. This summer salad bears the name of our chef, who has adapted it. A chef at the president of the Tunisian Republic's residence, Fethi Tounsi is also head chef of the Abou Nawas El Mechtel restaurants in Tunis.

Consisting mainly of chiles and tomatoes, *renga* salad is a very refreshing appetizer. It may seem surprising to find herrings in Tunisian cuisine. However, in the past, the inhabitants of the Goulette quarter, a small seaside resort near Tunis, stored these fish during the month of Ramadan. Although this tradition has tended to disappear, *renga* are still popular for their oily, flavorsome flesh.

According to how long they are soaked or cured, you find semi-salted smoked herrings and mild smoked herrings. The latter constitutes the bulk of the smoked herring market. Herrings have many similarities with sardines and mackerel, which can be used instead of herrings. If this is the case, blanch them first when you prepare this appetizer.

The chef uses capers as the main flavoring. The caper shrub is a spiny small tree growing wild in Tunisia from which the flower buds are picked. The smaller the capers used, the more subtle the flavor and the stronger the aroma.

The presence of the green and red chiles makes this appetizer relatively spicy. In Tunisia, there are numerous varieties of chiles which can be bought fresh or dried. The spicy flavor of these vegetables comes from a substance called "capsine." Capsine makes you salivate and stimulates the digestion. If you would prefer a milder flavor, remove the seeds and the whitish membranes inside.

Fethi Tounsi's *renga* salad is simple to make. In this recipe, herrings complement the Mediterranean flavors perfectly.

Wash the green and red chiles. Remove the stalks and seeds. Dice them. Wash the tomatoes, scoop them out and dice.

Brown the diced chiles and tomatoes in 7 tbsp (100 ml) of the olive oil.

Season the mixture with salt and pepper. Add the coriander, cumin, and crushed garlic cloves. Simmer for 3 minutes.

Renga Salad

Prepare the herring rosettes by cutting the fillets. Slice them into rectangular shapes. Place the trimmings to one side.

Chop up the herring trimmings and add to the chile and tomato mixture.

Pour the mixture into a salad bowl. Add the capers and the rest of the olive oil. Arrange the renga salad on a plate with a herring rosette in the center. Garnish with the olives and mint leaves, if using.

Tunisian

Preparation time: 40 minutes
Cooking time: 12 minutes
Difficulty: ★

Serves 4

1	cucumber
2	tomatoes
1	green bell pepper
1	red bell pepper
1	apple
1	onion
1/2	lemon

3 1/2 tbsp/50 ml	olive oil
1 pinch	dried mint
2	eggs
5 oz/150 g	tuna in oil
	salt and pepper

For the garnish:

12	pitted black olives
	fresh mint leaves
	(optional)

This cold appetizer is part of the Tunisian culinary heritage. Consisting of diced raw vegetables, it is particularly popular in the summer. Although it is very easy to make, it does however call for patience and attention to detail. It is essential to finely dice the vegetables to enjoy their freshness to the full.

The most popular Tunisian salads are: *mechouia*, made from broiled mild chiles and tomatoes; *houria*, consisting of cooked carrots; and this Tunisian salad, with the combined flavors of cucumber, bell peppers, tomatoes, and apple.

Tunisians use the Arab expression *wild el gambra* to describe cucumbers. This poetic metaphor means "son of the moon" because of the influence of this silvery heavenly body on their growth. Produced by a creeping annual plant of the melon and giant zucchini family (Cucurbitaceous plant), like zucchini and gherkins, the cucumber is a native

plant of the Himalayas. It can be served salted, raw, or cooked. Cucumber are fleshy, very firm, and long, with a pale-green, crisp, slightly bitter flesh and a thin, bright-green, and generally smooth skin. Our chef recommends that you taste the cucumber before mixing it with the salad. Some cucumbers can be a little bitter, and it would be a pity if this taste dominated the sweet taste of the bell peppers and the fragrance of the tomatoes and mint. If you choose a tart variety of apple, there's no need to season the salad with lemon juice.

Tunisian tuna in oil, an ingredient of this salad, is well known. Catching these migratory fish is an industrial and scientific procedure today, with shoals being located by helicopter. The tuna's head and spine are removed and the fish is boiled for a short time or steamed. Then it is dried, cut up, and boned. Before soaking it again in oil, the pieces are often flaked.

Peel the cucumber and remove the seeds. Wash the tomatoes and the bell peppers, and deseed them. Peel the apple and the onion.

Finely dice all the fruit and vegetables.

Mix all the ingredients in a bowl.

Salad

Prepare the salad seasoning of salt, pepper, lemon juice, and 3¹/₂ tbsp (50 ml) olive oil. Add a pinch of dried mint. Mix well.

Bring some salted water to the boil in a saucepan. Gently immerse the eggs in the saucepan and cook for about 12 minutes. Shell them and cut them in half lengthwise. Then cut into quarters.

Place the salad in a ramekin and turn it out onto the plate in the shape of a timbale. Add the eggs and the flaked tuna. Decorate with the olives and mint leaves, if using.

Slatet

Preparation time: 15 minutes
Cooking time: 30 minutes
Difficulty: ★

Serves 4

4   small bell peppers
2   small tomatoes
2   eggs
3½ tbsp/50 g   Swiss cheese
½   crystallized lemon
2 oz/50 g   canned tuna, drained
3½ tbsp/50 g   black olives
1   stale baguette
1 tbsp   capers
                       salt and pepper

Mechouia salad:
1 tbsp   harissa
1   garlic clove, chopped
1 tsp/5 g   tomato paste
3 tbsp/40 ml   vinegar
2 tbsp/30 ml   olive oil
1 pinch   caraway seeds

Making this specialty from the Tunis region is a good way of using up slightly stale bread. Tunisians either serve it as a snack with an aperitif, or as a cold appetizer. There are many variations on the theme of the famous *slatet blanquite*. Sabri Kouki's recipe is festive and very colorful. This recipe will appeal to anyone who creates imaginative meals with leftovers.

This age-old dish was documented in the 19th century in the book entitled *L'Inauguration du port de Tunis* (The Inauguration of the Port of Tunis), published in 1896. The *slatet blanquite* is also sometimes called *t'barua* (tavern), because it was also served as an appetizer. Formerly, the recipe was made with *ghalit*, a bread without much soft part. Nowadays, it's made with an ordinary baguette.

The canapés produced by Sabri Kouki are one of the main features of Tunisian *mechouia* salad. The bell peppers were traditionally cooked over a charcoal grill, but here the chef uses an oven broiler. After the bell peppers (or "steer horns" as they are known in Tunisia) are broiled, place them in a plastic bag. If you can, use zipped freezer bags—they have a closer seal. Their skin will lift and they'll be easy to peel.

Lovers of spicy food can substitute hot chiles for the bell peppers. In fact, it is not uncommon for Tunisians to call peppers what westerners call chiles.

If you buy very garlicky harissa, miss out the garlic clove in this recipe. The chef recommends that you use rather soft, stale bread, as the bread will soak up the sauce more easily. Another tip is to pinch the baguette slices before soaking them in the sauce. As soon as they've regained their initial shape, remove them immediately. They should be thoroughly saturated with the delicious liquid.

Broil the bell peppers and tomatoes in the oven for 20 minutes. Mix the harissa, chopped garlic, and tomato paste in a bowl. Put the cooked, warm, bell peppers in a plastic bag for 5 minutes.

Mix the harissa paste, tomatoes, and garlic with 1 cup (250 ml) of water. Add the vinegar and olive oil. Season the sauce with salt and pepper and add the caraway seeds.

Hard-boil the eggs. Remove the bell peppers and tomatoes from the bag. Peel them. Dice the Swiss cheese.

Blanquite

Chop the bell peppers finely, and cut the tomatoes into regular pieces. Cut up the crystallized fruit into small triangles. Flake the canned tuna. Cut the black olives in two. Place these ingredients to one side.

Shell the hard-boiled eggs and reduce them to crumbs, by sieving them. Cut the baguette into 1³/₄ in (4 cm) thick slices. Soak the slices in the sauce on both sides.

Top the slices of bread with the mechouia salad, a lemon triangle, tuna flakes, olives, capers, and diced Swiss cheese. Sprinkle them with hard-boiled egg. Allow 3 canapés per person.

T'Bikha

Preparation time:	25 minutes
Cooking time:	55 minutes
To soak the garbanzo beans:	12 hours
Difficulty:	★

Serves 4

2	onions
²/₃ cup/150 ml	olive oil
½ cup/100 g	garbanzo beans (chickpeas), soaked overnight and drained
1 tbsp/17 g	tomato paste

1 tbsp	harissa
1 tsp	paprika
1¼ lb/500 g	squash
2	tomatoes
5 oz/150 g	hot green chiles
5 oz/150 g	fava beans (broad beans)
4	garlic cloves, crushed salt and pepper

For the garnish:

	chopped parsley

T'bikha is a typical Tunisian specialty. This hot appetizer is served as the main course for many family meals. Although it varies from region to region, using different vegetables such as zucchini, carrots, or even eggplants, the most popular is most probably t'bikha with squash.

Called *kla* by the Tunisians, squash is the generic name for the fleshy fruit of any of the various plants of the gourd family (genus *Cucurbita*). These vegetables originally came from America, and were discovered through the expeditions of Christopher Columbus. At that time, gourd was reputed to be a remedy for "dryness of the tongue" and they were mainly eaten for their moisturizing properties. Spherical and bulky in shape, the gourd is distinguished by the yellow or red color of its skin and flesh.

This vegetarian dish also includes fava beans, which are a very common ingredient in Tunisian cuisine. Originally from Persia and Africa, they have been popular in the Mediterranean region since ancient times. When they are young, the delicate skin of fava beans does not need to be removed.

Fava beans are excellent spring and summer vegetables. They are prepared either hot or cold in a salad. In the *t'bikha*, their strong flavor is brought out. Our chef advises you to add them to the mixture once the garbanzo beans are cooked.

Don't forget to add a touch of chopped parsley as a garnish. Its aroma and color will give this recipe a dainty touch.

Peel the onions and cut them roughly into thin slices.

Sweat the onions in ²/₃ cup (150 ml) olive oil. Add the garbanzo beans and the tomato paste. Mix well.

Season with salt and pepper. Add the harissa and the paprika. Stir and cover with water. Cook for approximately 25 minutes.

with Gourd

Peel and cut the squash and tomatoes into large cubes. Cut the hot chiles in two, deseed and cut into small pieces.

Shell the fava beans. Remove the skin of the beans and add the beans to the mixture.

Stir the pieces of squash, tomatoes, and chiles into the saucepan. Cook for approximately 20 minutes. Five minutes before the end of the cooking time, add the crushed garlic cloves. Pour the t'bikha into a deep dish and garnish with a little chopped parsley.

Trio of Tunisian

Preparation time:	40 minutes
Cooking time:	25 minutes
Difficulty:	★★

Serves 4

4	fritter sheets
1	lemon
	cooking oil

For the basic filling:

1 medium-sized	onion, chopped
4 tbsp/50 ml	olive oil
½ bunch	parsley
1 x 5 oz/150 g	potato, cooked and puréed

3½ tbsp/50 g	capers, chopped
1	egg
	salt and pepper

For the chicken filling:

3½ oz/100 g	chicken breast meat
1 tsp	ground coriander

For the ground meat filling:

3½ oz/100 g	ground beef
1 tbsp	olive oil
1 tsp	ground coriander
1 tsp	turmeric
1 tsp	caraway seeds

For the tuna filling:

½ can	tuna in oil, drained

For the garnish:

	paprika (optional)

When you think of Tunisia you immediately picture beautiful landscapes, fine sandy beaches, and … its delicious fritters! They are a national specialty that is enjoyed at any time of day.

Fritter sheets, which are also called *malsouka*, are a legacy of the Turks' passage through Tunisia. These "crepes," which are sheets of unleavened fine semolina, are traditionally prepared on a tinned copper tray, placed over a stove. Every Tunisian family chooses its own fritter fillings, according to taste, season, or budget. Some families fill them with liver pâté, red snapper, or even shrimp. But for the most part, they're made with tuna, eggs, or meat.

In fact, you can use any ingredients you like for this recipe. However, to make this specialty properly you must include the basic filling, which is always made of onion, chopped parsley, egg, and potato. Some people also like to add

capers, which are young flower buds from the caper shrub and are generally pickled in white vinegar or brine. Used as a flavoring, capers were very popular with the ancient Romans when they occupied Tunisia.

Different shapes of fritters can be served. The chef suggests that you make a trio of triangle, cigar, and half-moon shapes. He suggests that you fill them with tuna in oil, which is a great favorite of the Tunisians, or with chicken breast. If you make them with ground meat, as in this recipe, add a little water and season with spices halfway through cooking. Most importantly, don't forget to add the coriander (which is also called "Arabic parsley"), as its oriental aroma flavors the meat perfectly.

When they are served, the trio of Tunisian mini-fritters are like an invitation to travel and offer a taste of this warm and friendly country.

Prepare the basic filling by browning the chopped onions in the olive oil for about 5 minutes. Stir in the chopped parsley. Allow to cool. Add the potato purée and the chopped capers. Season with salt and pepper. Break the egg into the mixture. Stir and place to one side.

With a pair of scissors, cut 2 fritter sheets into 2½ in (6 cm) wide strips to make the triangles; cut another fritter sheet in 2 to make the cigars; using a pastry cutter, cut out circles in the other sheet, to make the half-moons.

Prepare the different fillings by cooking the ground meat in olive oil and spices; cook the chicken in salted water for 5 minutes, and chop it with the coriander. Flake the tuna. Share out the basic filling between each filling. Place a circle of each filling on each fritter sheet.

Mini-Fritters

Spread the chicken filling evenly at the end of the strip. Fold the fritters into triangles by rolling them once to the left, and once to the right, as if you're tucking them in.

Prepare the cigar fritters by placing the ground meat filling at the end of the sheet. Fold it once in a $^1/_2$ round towards the middle and roll it up to the end. For the half-moons, place a spoonful of the tuna filling on one side and pull the sheet over it.

Fry the fritters, 3 minutes on each side. Soak up any excess oil on a paper towel. Arrange a selection on plates, served with a lemon quarter, and dusted with paprika, if using.

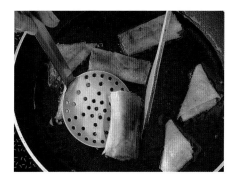

Soups &
Tagines

Berkoukech from

Preparation time:	20 minutes	1 tbsp	mild paprika
Cooking time:	1 hour 5 minutes	1 tbsp/17 g	tomato paste
For the sorghum		4	dried red chiles
to rise:	12 hours	3½ tbsp/50 ml	olive oil
For the fava beans			salt
to soak:	12 hours		
Difficulty:	★		

Serves 4

7 oz/200 g	carrots
1	fresh onion
7 oz/200 g	turnips
6	spinach leaves
½	white cabbage

7 oz/200 g dried fava beans (broad beans), soaked

For the batter:

2 lb 10 oz/1.2 kg	ground sorghum
6 tsp/30 g	yeast (if using active dry yeast, follow maker's instructions)
250 ml	tepid water
1 pinch	sugar
1	lemon

Berkoukech from Dar-Chaabane is an excellent winter dish. This traditional peasant soup consists of seasonal vegetables—carrots, turnips, fava beans, cabbages, and so on. Farmers generally eat it at the end of the morning.

Rafik Tlatli discovered this recipe at the house of a friend's mother, who was born in Dar-Chaabane. This small village, 1¼ miles (2 kilometers) from Nabeul in the Cap Bon region, is renowned for its stone-cutters. These artisans produce door frames for buildings in many Tunisian towns. Their sculpted motifs are recognizable by their stylized geometric figures or plants.

The presence of risen sorghum in the *berkoukech* makes a nourishing meal of this soup. This cereal (also called heavy millet) has been cultivated since ancient times. Documents dating back to 1,900 BC show that the Indians had made it one of their staple foods. In some Tunisian families, sorghum is served at breakfast. Called *droâ*, it is blended with milk and cinnamon. To enhance the slightly sharp taste of this soup, you may like to follow the example of our chef and add a touch of lemon juice.

If you like, Swiss chard can be substituted for the spinach leaves. To enrich the soup, some villagers add chicken or *kadid*, which is lamb dried in the sun and preserved in olive oil. Dried red chiles are an essential ingredient for the spicy flavor they bring, and so is ground paprika.

Berkoukech from Dar-Chaabane is an original, authentic recipe. As it is not very well known by Tunisians, there is a danger it will eventually be forgotten. Rafik Tlatli wants to popularize it so that it remains a part of the culinary heritage of his country.

Prepare the sorghum the day before by pouring 7 oz (200 g) sorghum into a bowl. Make a well and incorporate the yeast. Pour over 250 ml tepid water and a pinch of sugar. Stir with a spatula and leave the mixture to rise over a period of 12 hours.

Peel the carrots and the onion. Wash the turnips and remove the tops. Cut up the vegetables roughly. Thinly slice the spinach leaves and the cabbage, and drain the soaked fava beans.

Pour boiling water into the couscous steamer until it is three-quarters full and add all the vegetables, except the cabbage. Cook for 15 minutes. Add the cabbage. Season with salt, paprika, and tomato paste. Stir in the whole chiles. Cook for about 40 minutes.

Dar-Chaabane

Pour 2 lb 3 oz (1 kg) of sorghum into a large container and add the risen sorghum mixture.

Knead the mixture with your hands until well mixed. Add the lemon juice and if necessary a little water.

When the vegetables are cooked, add the sorghum. Boil for 10 minutes, while stirring with a wooden spoon until you have a smooth soup with a few lumps. Pour the berkoukech into deep plates and trickle olive oil over it.

Chorba with

Preparation time: 35 minutes
Cooking time: 30 minutes
Difficulty: ★

Serves 4

1	onion, finely chopped
4 tbsp/50 ml	olive oil
5 tbsp/100 g	tomato paste
1	celery stick, chopped
1	sprig parsley, chopped

1¼ lb/500 g	sole, red snapper, and bream
1¼ cups/250 g	short pasta ("langues d'oiseaux"—"birds' tongues")
	salt and pepper

For the garnish:

	parsley
2	lemons, quartered

In Arabic, *chorba* means a soup. With this recipe, Chedly Azzaz introduces a coastal region specialty. *Chorba* with Mediterranean fish is simply a Tunisian fish soup. Traditionally, this popular dish used less expensive fish such as scorpion fish and whiting, cut into pieces and added to the stock. Occasionally, some families add the head of a grouper fish.

Our chef devised this sole, bream, and small red snapper soup as a *chorba* for feast days. Red snappers have a unique flavor, and their fine, delicate flesh makes them a great favorite. So as not to mask their flavor, no spices have been added. However, in the Sfax region, this dish is made with cumin. If you want a spicier flavor, add a tablespoon of harissa. You can also add lemon juice to the stock.

The strong aroma of the celery stick works its way through the *chorba* during cooking. Its flavor is akin to fennel. Also used for its distinctive fragrance, the characteristic flavor of flat-leaf parsley permeates the soup. This aromatic plant is sold all year round. Parsley must be very green and fresh, and the leaves and stalks rigid.

According to legend, the Arabs expelled from Spain after the fall of Granada took back pasta with them, which was previously unknown in North Africa. This new ingredient, a legacy of the Arab-Andalucian world, has found its place in Tunisian culinary heritage, and in particular in the *chorba*. You can use short macaroni instead of *"langues d'oiseaux"* ("birds' tongues"—short pasta), which are typical of the Orient.

Originally prepared during the month of Ramadan, today *chorba* has become a popular, very fashionable dish. So popular, indeed, that some families may eat it two or three times a week!

Sweat the chopped onions in a pan with the olive oil, without browning, for approximately 4 minutes.

Add the tomato paste, half the chopped celery and half the chopped parsley to the pan. Place the rest to one side. Season with salt and pepper. Sweat for another 2 minutes.

Add cold water to the mixture.

Mediterranean Fish

Wash, scale, gut, and clean the fish. Cut them up into large pieces. Add them to the pan and cook uncovered for 15 minutes. Remove the cooked fish and place to one side.

Pour in a little water. Adjust the seasoning. Add the short pasta and cook for approximately 15 minutes.

Strip the flesh from the fish, and remove the bones. Add the rest of the chopped parsley and celery to the soup. Cook gently for a further 2 minutes. Add the fish meat. Serve the chorba in a soup tureen and garnish with parsley. Put the quartered lemons in a separate dish.

Dchich

Preparation time:	10 minutes
Cooking time:	50 minutes
To soak the octopus and garbanzo beans:	24 hours
Difficulty:	★

Serves 4

2 oz/50 g	dried octopus
3½ tbsp/50 g	Egyptian fava beans (broad beans)
1	onion, chopped
2	garlic cloves, chopped
3 tbsp/ 40 ml	olive oil
2 tbsp/35 g	tomato paste
1 tsp	harissa

1 tsp	allspice
¼ cup/50 g	garbanzo beans (chickpeas)
¾ cup/150 g	bulgur wheat
½ bunch	parsley, chopped
1	celery top, chopped
	salt and pepper

This soup is one of the specialties of Monastir. It's served extensively when the sun is unpredictable and winter is on its way with a vengeance. During the hot season, the fishermen of this charming town stock up on octopus, which is used to enhance the flavor of the *dchich*. The people of Monastir prefer to use small octopus for this famous recipe as their flesh is more delicate and tastier.

Every part of this small animal is edible! Blanching or soaking it overnight may be enough to tenderize it, but older octopuses are usually beaten to tenderize them. Octopuses are caught in spring at night, and are left to dry in the sun throughout the summer.

Bulgur wheat, the cereal used in this delicious winter soup, is crushed durum wheat. It's a highly nutritious food, and is a favorite accompaniment in Turkish dishes. It is a common dish in Tunisian homes, often accompanied by a very red tomato sauce. The crushed wheat soaks up all the sauce. In Mohamed Bouagga's recipe it doesn't take long for the cereal to absorb all the juices.

Imported from Egypt, as their name would suggest, Egyptian fava beans bring a different texture to the meal. In contrast to dried garbanzo beans, there's absolutely no need to pre-soak dried fava beans. You can also use fresh ones instead; they'll cook quicker. If the fava beans are young, don't remove their skin—they'll keep their flavor better. To make preparation easier, we recommend buying canned garbanzo beans, which are pre-cooked, require no prior soaking, and will cook more quickly.

Soak the octopus and the garbanzo beans the day before required. The next day, drain the octopus and the garbanzo beans. Dice the octopus and place to one side. Brown the onion and garlic in 3 tbsp of the olive oil.

Add the tomato paste, harissa, and allspice to the browned garlic and onion. Season with salt and pepper.

Add 8 cups (2 liters) of water. Cook the stock for approximately 5 minutes.

with Octopus

Add the garbanzo beans and the Egyptian fava beans to the stock.

Half-way through cooking the fava beans and garbanzo beans, add the diced octopus. Adjust the seasoning.

Then add the bulgur wheat. Simmer for approximately 30 minutes. Add the chopped parsley and celery top to the dchich when it's cooked. Serve very hot.

Ftir

Preparation time:	*1 hour*
Cooking time:	*40 minutes*
Difficulty:	★★

Serves 4

5 oz/150 g	carrots
5 oz/150 g	potatoes
1	celery heart
1	celery stick
8³/₄ oz/250 g	shoulder of lamb
3¹/₂ tbsp/50 ml	olive oil
1 pinch	saffron strands
1	onion, sliced
³/₄ cup/100g	peas
	cooking oil

For the cigar fritters:

3¹/₂ oz/100 g	ground lamb
2 tbsp/30 ml	olive oil
4 tsp/20 g	chopped parsley
5 tsp/25 g	grated Swiss cheese
2	eggs
2	*malsouka* sheets (fritter sheets)
1	egg yolk
¹/₂	lemon
	salt and pepper

Ftir el euch is a very substantial soup. Some Tunisian families eat it in the evening as a main course. Very rich in vegetables, Mohamed Boujelben suggests you serve this original specialty with small, cigar-shaped fritters—*malsouka* sheets filled with lamb.

For a successful soup, our chef recommends that you start by cooking the peas, celery, and carrots. Carrots are thought to have originally come from Central Asia. They are found in many Tunisian recipes and are packed with vitamin A. Select new carrots, which have an excellent flavor. They must be very hard, crunchy, blemish-free, and their tops should be green and fresh. They will keep for about two weeks in the refrigerator.

Ten minutes after you've started cooking, add the potatoes. Wait another ten minutes and remove the celery stick. This

kitchen garden plant is renowned for the wonderful flavor it gives to soups, sauces, and ragouts.

Almost at the end of the cooking time, you must add an egg yolk and lemon juice to the soup. Our chef advises you to blend them off the heat.

Ftir el euch is served with small cigar-shaped fritters. Stuffed with a filling, *malsouka* are closely associated with Tunisian culinary heritage. Made with all-purpose flour, salt, oil, and water, these sheets are used to prepare the famous *brick* (fritters). Our chef wanted to present the cigars in a separate dish. According to a family's taste, the fritters are sometimes cut up and served in the soup.

Ftir el euch is a meal in itself. It is an ideal dish for children as it is not spicy.

Peel and finely dice the carrots and potatoes.

Thinly slice the celery heart. Dice the celery stick.

Trim the shoulder of lamb and cut into cubes.

el Euch

Fry the lamb cubes gently in the olive oil. Soak the saffron in a little water and add the water with the sliced onion. Season with salt and pepper. Cover with water. Bring to the boil. Add carrots, peas, celery, and potatoes. Cook for 30 minutes.

Prepare the cigar fillings by browning the ground lamb in the olive oil. Season with salt and pepper. Add the chopped parsley, grated Swiss cheese, and 1 egg. Mix well. Beat the other egg.

To make the cigars, spread out the malsouka sheets and cut them in half. Place some filling along the curved side, and roll up. Stick down the edge with a little beaten egg. Fry the cigars in the cooking oil. Finally, mix 1 egg yolk and the juice of 1/2 lemon into the soup.

Hlalem

Preparation time:	30 minutes
Cooking time:	45 minutes
Difficulty:	★★

Serves 4

3½ oz/100 g	lamb
4	artichokes
2	lemons
4 tsp/20 ml	olive oil

1 bunch	celery, chopped
1 bunch	flat-leaf parsley, chopped
4 tsp/20 g	tomato paste
¼ cup/50 g	soaked garbanzo beans (chickpeas)
6½ tbsp/100 g	hlalem pasta
	salt and pepper

The inhabitants of Tunis are great consumers of *hlalem* throughout the year, but in spring they add a few delicious slices of artichoke to it. More often than not, this very substantial soup, using a minuscule type of pasta, is enriched with dried lamb or *kadid*. To make the recipe easier, Ali Matri has used fresh lamb, but there's nothing to stop you trying beef or veal instead.

The preparation of the *kadid* is actually quite complicated. During the feast of *Aïd*, pieces of lamb are set aside, for example from the low ribs that are cut up into strips. Rubbed with mint, garlic, chile, and salt, the meat is put out to dry in the sun for several days, and then fried in olive oil. Afterwards, it can be kept for several months. In the past, Tunisians didn't eat fresh meat every day, but they laid in reserves so that there was always some *kadid* throughout the year.

Artichokes bring their distinctive flavor to this *hlalem*. Two varieties—the green and the violet—are those favored by Tunisian gourmets. Ali Matri prefers the violet variety, which is more fragrant. When he prepares them, he always leaves the tendril root of the stem under the artichoke heart to flavor the soup. If the stems are very tender, peel them and cut up their hearts into small cubes. Add them to the soup just after the tomato paste. Spring *hlalem* can also be made with early fava beans or peas.

The small variety of pasta—*hlalem*—is the ingredient that gives this soup its character. *Hlalem* are minuscule, like fine grains of rice, and are prepared half with all-purpose flour and half with semolina enriched with brewer's yeast, and separated by hand. After cooking, they should still have the taste of the yeast, and be a little crumbly in the mouth.

Using a sharp knife, cut the lamb into slices, then into small regular cubes ½ in (1 cm) across.

Cut the artichoke stems at the base of the head. With a small pointed knife, remove the leaves and the beard. Squeeze half a lemon on to the hearts you have removed, to prevent them discoloring, then immerse in a bowl of cold water.

Rapidly brown the meat cubes in the olive oil in a stockpot. Season with salt and pepper, and stir to prevent it sticking to the bottom of the pan. Add the chopped celery and parsley. Cook for 10 minutes until the juice starts to run.

with Artichokes

Next, add a glass of cold water to the mixture. Boil gently until the herbs are very tender. Incorporate the tomato paste with a spatula. Stir, and leave to simmer so that the tomato loses its acidity.

Add a glass of cold water to the saucepan. Bring to the boil, then add the artichoke hearts cut into large strips and the garbanzo beans. Adjust the seasoning. Cook for approximately 10 minutes uncovered.

When the artichokes are nearly tender, add the hlalem pasta. Cook for another 5 to 10 minutes. Adjust the seasoning and serve hot. Serve with the remaining lemon cut into quarters.

Hsou from

Preparation time:	15 minutes
Cooking time:	40 minutes
Difficulty:	☆

Serves 4

1	onion, chopped
6½ tbsp/100 ml	olive oil
1 tbsp/17 g	tomato paste
1 tsp	harissa
1 tsp	paprika
1 tsp	caraway seeds
1 tsp	ground coriander

1	celery stick
3	garlic cloves, crushed
A few	rue leaves
½ cup/70 g	medium-sized semolina
1	lemon
	salt and pepper

For the garnish:

A few	rue leaves
	lemon slice

Tunisians generally use the word *hsou* when referring to a liquid mixture. This soup comes from the oasis of Tozeur, in the southwest of the country, and is particularly famous for its spiciness. Eaten with stale bread in the morning by the *ramess*, the date harvesters, *hsou* is an ideal start to the day and helps to keep out the cold.

This popular Tozeur dish is also prepared during the period of fasting—Ramadan. In some families, it is served in the evening after prayers, with milk and a few dates.

This meatless soup is full of spices and aromatic plants. One of them, rue, grows wild in this region, close to the Sahara desert. The small tree, resembling a herbaceous perennial, grows to about 23–29 in (60–75 cm) high. Covered in round, serrated leaves, with a green or bluish-green color, rue is recognizable by its strong, bitter

scent. Use the leaves sparingly in this recipe, and be aware that some people may have an allergic reaction to it. It's not essential to include it. On the other hand, the celery stick is definitely needed. Finely chopped, it gives this soup a pleasant flavor. Available in the markets all the year round, celery should be very green, perfectly hard, blemish-free, with no yellowish marks at the base. The very tender heart of this vegetable is delicious raw.

Semolina gives body to this peasant dish. After adding it to the saucepan, our chef advises that you skim the vegetable fat off the soup.

Easy to make, *hsou* from the oases will be popular with those who love spicy flavors. Try this dish to discover the culinary traditions of this region of Tunisia.

Gently fry the chopped onion in the olive oil.

Stir in the tomato paste, harissa, paprika, caraway seeds, and coriander. Season with salt and pepper. Stir well with a wooden spatula.

Wash and chop the celery. Add the celery and the crushed garlic cloves to the mixture.

the Oases

Add 4 cups (1 liter) water. Stir well and cook for approximately 20 minutes.

Wash the rue leaves and add them to the soup mixture. Add the semolina and stir. Cook for approximately 10 minutes.

Peel the lemon thoroughly. Dice the pulp very finely, remove the pits and add the lemon cubes to the mixture. Cook for a further 5 minutes. Pour the soup into a dish. Garnish with rue leaves and 1 lemon slice.

Lahmet

Preparation time:	*10 minutes*
Cooking time:	*40 minutes*
Difficulty:	✶

Serves 4

4	potatoes
1¾ lb/800 g	beef fillets in 4 slices
1 tbsp	capers
10 tbsp/150 g	large green olives
1	egg
6½ tbsp/100 g	grated Swiss cheese
	salt and pepper
	allspice

For the mechouia salad:

2	green bell peppers
2	red bell peppers
2	tomatoes

For the tomato sauce:

2½ cups/500 g	tomatoes, chopped
1	garlic clove
1	onion
1 tbsp/17 g	tomato paste
1 tbsp	harissa
2½ tbsp/40 ml	olive oil

This is a typically Tunisian recipe and the name means "meat in salad." In Sabri Kouki's recipe, the famous *mechouia* salad accompanies this dish. In the past, this dish was made with the cheese "gouta"; nowadays, *lahmet slata* is made with Swiss cheese, which has a better consistency when cooked.

The decoration of this dish is very elaborate, because even though this is a family dish (or even rustic) it must also be pleasing to the eye. This recipe is cooked slowly with fillet or rump steak. Select very tender meat. As an alternative and a break from tradition, Sabri Kouki suggests using turkey escalopes. In this case, make sure you reduce the cooking time, especially if the meat is thin.

The "allspice" in the *lahmet slata* is characteristic of this recipe, with its delicately proportioned mix of ground pepper, caraway seeds, coriander, and ground cinnamon. Add the allspice at the end of cooking to avoid a pungent taste.

Mechouia salad is a great classic, a veritable institution in Tunisian cuisine. It is made locally with "steer horns"— small and fairly long, green or red, and sweet bell peppers. As an alternative, you can make this recipe with square-shaped bell peppers, which are much easier to find.

The potato purée can be flavored, according to the contents of your larder, either with tuna or capers. For a smoother flavor, add 1 tbsp (15 ml) olive oil.

For the mechouia *salad: setting aside 1 piece of green and red bell pepper, broil the bell peppers and tomatoes under the oven grill for 15–20 minutes. Once cooked, seal in a plastic bag for 5 minutes. Peel, then chop finely.*

Cook the potatoes in salted water for 15 minutes. Drain and keep hot to one side. Prepare the tomato sauce: brown the chopped tomatoes, garlic, and onion with the tomato paste and harissa in 2½ tbsp (40 ml) olive oil. Cook for 10 minutes.

Tenderize the beef slices. Add the beef slices to the sauce with the capers. Season with salt and pepper. Strain the potatoes through a vegetable mill. Keep this purée hot.

Slata

Add ¾ cup (200 ml) water to the meat. Add 2 pinches of allspice. Cook over a low heat until the oil rises to the surface. Preheat your oven at 430 °F/220 °C.

Blend the hot potato purée with the mechouia salad. Add 1 egg and the grated Swiss cheese. Adjust the seasoning. Cut the reserved green and red bell peppers into thin slices. Set aside.

Arrange the beef slices in a cake mold, put a layer of purée on top and then a layer of the meat sauce. Top with the meat and mechouia. Remove the mold and bake in the oven for 5 to 10 minutes, until the purée lightly browns. Garnish with the reserved bell pepper strips and capers. Serve hot.

Minina

Preparation time:	*25 minutes*
Cooking time:	*1 hour 20 minutes*
Difficulty:	☆

Serves 4

1	lamb's brain
1½ lb/700 g	chicken
7 tbsp/100 ml	Tunisian olive oil
7 oz/200 g	onions, chopped
1 tbsp/20 g	chopped garlic
1 pinch	saffron strands
1 tsp ground	cumin
4 or 5	peppercorns
1	bay leaf
10	eggs
4 slices	sandwich bread
1 pinch	ground allspice
	table salt
	unsalted butter for greasing

In Tunisian Jewish families, *minina* is served at notable occasions: engagements, marriages, circumcisions, *bar mitzvah* … and to honor guests. A symbol of prosperity and celebration, this dish is always served with a *kemia*, a selection of colorful small dishes garnished with turnips marinated in harissa, olives, fennel, tuna, carrots, or cucumber.

These delicacies, a random collection, are usually served with fig brandy or *boukha*. During the "aperitif," the oldest person present takes some of the food, and offers it to the circle of family and friends, inviting each guest to partake. This gesture is still performed today in Jewish families of Tunisian origin, wherever they live. Neighboring Muslim families have also adopted the custom.

In contrast to other Tunisian tagines, thickened with cheese as well as eggs, the *minina* blends the flavors of saffron chicken, lamb's brains, and eggs. Without the cheese, the texture is much lighter. As lamb's brain is tender and delicate, it is the most suitable ingredient for the *minina*. Some cooks do also prepare it without the brain.

You can bone a whole chicken and use all the meat, or prepare it with escalopes, which cook quickly. Thoroughly reduce them in the saffron water and regularly add more water. When the chicken is cooked, add the rest of the saffron water and blend with the stock to make a sauce. Once filtered, the sauce is thickened with starch and served in a sauceboat.

The addition of bread soaked in water or milk is optional, but it gives the *minina* a risen appearance. Similarly, our chef's advice is to regularly moisten the dish with saffron water while it's baking in the oven, to improve its texture and flavor.

Rinse the lamb's brain thoroughly, and drain it. Cut up the chicken. Remove the fillets and the meat from the thighs. Finely cut it all into small cubes.

Heat the oil in a saucepan. Add the onions, garlic, and chicken to the hot oil and cook until golden brown, while stirring.

Bring a small saucepan of water to the boil. Sprinkle saffron into it. Boil for 5 minutes. Baste the chicken mixture several times with a ladle of saffron water, until it is cooked. Filter, and place the ingredients and juice separately to one side. Use this juice to make the sauce as described.

Heat a saucepan of water with cumin, peppercorns, and a bay leaf. Place the pieces of brain in the hot water, ensuring they're covered, and poach.

Hard-boil 3 of the eggs for 10 minutes. Shell them and chop up the whites. Crumble the bread and soak in water or milk. Add the finely diced brain, chopped egg whites, bread, allspice, and salt to the chicken terrine. Thoroughly mix this tagine filling.

Break 7 eggs into the tagine. Line a loaf tin with buttered greaseproof paper. Fill with the tagine. Cover with tinfoil. Bake in the oven for 45 minutes in a tray filled with hot water. Serve in slices, with the saffron sauce in a separate dish.

Bey's

Preparation time:	30 minutes
Cooking time:	20 minutes
Difficulty:	★

Serves 4

2 lb/1 kg	spinach
9	eggs
10 tbsp/150 g	ricotta
10 tbsp/150 g	grated Swiss cheese
6½ tbsp/100 g	parsley, chopped
1 tbsp	olive oil

For the basic filling:

8¾ oz/250 g	ground lamb
7 tbsp/100 ml	olive oil
1	onion, chopped
3	garlic cloves, crushed
1 large pinch	ground coriander
	salt and pepper

In the Tunisian culinary tradition, the tagine resembles a kind of "tart." It is nothing like the Moroccan dish of the same name. According to family and region, this popular dish, made from eggs and grated cheese, is served with various vegetables and meats.

Very easy to make, *Bey's tagine* is our chef's version. Three fillings, blended separately with the basic filling, make this a sophisticated and original dish. Adopting a similar presentation to the *baklawa el bey*, a tri-colored marzipan sweetmeat, Mohamed Boujelben has reworked the famous tagine by experimenting with colors and shapes.

The name of this recipe is an allusion to Tunisian history, and in particular to the Ottoman presence. The *bey*, a Turkish governor of a province or district in the service of the sultan, was in charge of administration until the 18th century. Numerous palace conspiracies led to this title becoming hereditary, and later to the foundation of the Husseinite dynasty.

Famous for their gastronomic mores, the *beys* would no doubt have appreciated their title being given to this tagine. Blended with the basic filling of ground lamb, the spinach forms the first layer of this dish. Originating from Persia, spinach may be eaten raw in a salad or cooked. The leaves must be well-shaped, complete, and unblemished. Before blanching them, our chef recommends washing them in running water, without soaking them.

The central part is cheese-based, making a contrasting white layer, setting off the green of the spinach and parsley layers. Made with grated Swiss cheese and ricotta, this filling brings a light, smooth flavor to the dish.

Make the basic filling by gently frying the ground lamb in the olive oil. Add the chopped onion and the crushed garlic. Season with salt and pepper. Add the coriander. Mix well. Allow to cool and place to one side.

Blanch the spinach in boiling water for approximately 3 minutes then drain. Shape the spinach into small bundles and chop it up.

Separate the basic filling into 3 equal parts. Prepare the spinach filling by mixing it with 3 of the eggs and one part of the basic filling.

Tagine

Prepare the cheese filling by mixing the ricotta and grated Swiss cheese with 3 more eggs and the second batch of basic filling.

Prepare the third filling by mixing the chopped parsley with the remaining 3 eggs and the rest of the basic filling.

Grease the dish with 1 tbsp olive oil and spread the spinach filling over it. Bake in the oven at 350 °F/180 °C for 5 minutes. Spread the cheese filling over. Bake again for 5 minutes. Top with the parsley filling. Bake again for 5 minutes. Cool, and turn out. Cut into diamond shapes.

Blanched Wheat Soup

Preparation time:	20 minutes
Cooking time:	55 minutes
To soak the garbanzo beans and lentils:	12 hours
Difficulty:	★

Serves 6

4 tbsp/50 ml	Tunisian olive oil
½ cup/100 g	bulgur wheat
3½ oz/100 g	green fava beans (broad beans), peeled
¼ cup/50 g	garbanzo beans (chickpeas), soaked overnight
1 oz/30 g	lentils, soaked overnight
2	onions, chopped
4 tbsp/70 g	tomato paste
5 tsp/25 g	harissa
5 tsp/25 g	mild paprika
5 tsp/25 g	caraway seeds
4 cloves	garlic, crushed
1	carrot
1	turnip
6 tsp/30 g	peas
½ bunch	flat-leaf parsley
½ bunch	fresh coriander
10	spinach leaves
2	celery sticks
1 or 2	lemons
	salt and pepper

In Tunisia, blanched wheat soup with vegetables is called *borghol jeri bil khodhra*. *Borghol* is a product made from cooked wheat (bulgur); *jeri* means "liquid preparation"; *khodhra* is a general term for vegetables. This nourishing vegetarian dish, with its assortment of pulses, is a perfect soup to warm you up in the winter.

Tunisians wisely use a large variety of dried vegetables in their diet: they serve garbanzo beans, fava beans, and lentils daily. After the harvest, the vegetables are dried in the sun, to be preserved for the year. In this country, lentils are eaten in salads as well as in main courses, for instance cooked with pieces of lamb. Tunisians also enjoy garbanzo beans cooked in beef stock, flavored with olive oil, cumin, and harissa at breakfast.

For his soup, our chef trims the vegetables and finely chops them into regular pieces. He is careful to stagger the cooking times, so that all the diced vegetables keep their shape, texture, and flavor. In the past, Tunisian grandmothers cooked them all simultaneously.

In winter, dried fava beans are used in this soup, but are replaced here by green fava beans for their fresh color. Like lentils and garbanzo beans, you need to soak the dried beans overnight. Of course, the quantity and assortment of vegetables will vary according to the season and regional availability. Tunisians serve lemon quarters with this soup, which they squeeze onto their plate just before eating the meal.

On Kerkenah, the native island of our chef, people like to dip a piece of round, flat, *galit* bread, which is full of holes, in their *borghol* with vegetables. They dry the bread out in the open air on nets hanging against the walls of their houses.

Fill a saucepan with 8 cups (2 liters) water and a trickle of olive oil. Pour in the bulgur wheat, fava beans, garbanzo beans, lentils, and chopped onions. Cook for 30 minutes.

Then add the tomato paste, harissa, paprika, salt, pepper, caraway seeds, and garlic to the vegetables. Cook for a further 10 minutes over a low heat.

Peel the turnip and carrot, and cut into small regular cubes. Add these to the soup.

with Vegetables

Then add the peas to the soup. Cook for a further 5 minutes.

On a chopping board, chop the parsley, coriander, spinach, and then the celery sticks.

Add these to the soup. Stop cooking after another 7–10 minutes. Adjust the seasoning. Serve hot, with lemon quarters.

Eggplant and

Preparation time: 35 minutes
Cooking time: 1 hour 20 minutes
Difficulty: ★

Serves 4

1¼ lb/500 g	boned shoulder of lamb
14 oz/400 g	eggplants
1	large onion, chopped
7 tbsp/100 ml	olive oil
1 pinch	turmeric
½ bunch	parsley, chopped
13 tbsp/200 g	grated cheese
8	eggs
	cooking oil
	salt and pepper

The culinary heritage of Tunisia reflects its history. Invaded several times, the population of this country has assimilated the culinary traditions of its occupying forces over the centuries. Eggplant and lamb tagine is evidence of this cultural integration. This dish, originating from the time of the Ottoman Empire, was mainly served at the tables of the affluent classes in Tunis until the 1960s. Since then, it has become more widely popular and is enjoyed by many families.

The tagine takes its name from the deep, terracotta, glazed pot, with a well-sealed conical lid, in which it is prepared. This pot can be used to cook and serve slow-cooking dishes, keeping them moist and flavorsome. The word "tagine" usually means vegetables, fish, poultry, or meat prepared in this way. But the Tunisian tagine is very different, and is actually a kind of "tart" made from eggs and grated cheese, mixed with meat and various vegetables.

To be designated as lamb, the animal must be no more than 300 days old at the time of slaughter. If you prefer, you can use beef or veal. When you season the meat, try adding a little harissa to pep up the flavor.

Eggplants are strongly flavored and are an ingredient of many oriental and Mediterranean dishes. They are thought to originally come from the Indo-Burmese region. For the tagine, cut the eggplants into cubes.

Our chef has used turmeric for its irreplaceable aroma. This herbaceous plant is generally used as a spice or for coloring. The turmeric root, after grinding, has a slightly sharper flavor than saffron.

In Tunisia, eggplant and lamb tagine is mainly eaten during the month of Ramadan. This delicious dish is enjoyed in the evening under the benevolent gaze of the moon…

Trim the lamb and cut it into small pieces. Wash the eggplants and cut them into thin slices.

Brown the chopped onion in 3½ tbsp (50 ml) of the olive oil. Add the lamb pieces. Fry gently. Season with salt and pepper and stir in the turmeric.

Add sufficient water to the mixture to just cover it. Cook uncovered until the stock has completely evaporated. Add the chopped parsley. Allow to cool.

Lamb Tagine

Break the eggs into a bowl and beat them. Stir into the meat mixture. Add 10 tbsp (150 g) of the grated cheese. Stir well to combine.

Gently fry the eggplant slices in the cooking oil. Absorb excess oil on a paper towel. Stir them gently but thoroughly into the mixture.

Grease the mold with the remaining olive oil. Empty the tagine into the mold and sprinkle the rest of the cheese over it. Bake in the oven at 350 °F/180 °C for approximately 25 minutes. Turn out the tagine with the help of a spatula and arrange on a dish.

Royal Crown

Preparation time:	15 minutes
Cooking time:	35 minutes
For the batter to stand:	30 minutes
Difficulty:	☆

Serves 4

8³/₄ oz/250 g	raw shrimp
1¹/₄ lb/500 g	shelled shrimp
10 tbsp/150 g	grated Swiss cheese
11	eggs
3¹/₂ tbsp/50 g	large green olives
¹/₂ tsp	cumin
1 tbsp	chopped tomatoes
1 tbsp (15 ml)	olive oil

| | cooking oil |
| | salt and pepper |

For the tartare sauce:

2	egg yolks
1 tsp	prepared mustard
generous 1 cup/250 ml	sunflower oil
1 tsp	chopped capers
1 tsp	chopped parsley
1 tsp	chopped onion
1 tsp	chopped hard-boiled egg

For the batter:

⁷/₈ cup/100 g	all-purpose flour
1 cup/250 ml	beer
1	egg

This golden crown is indeed royal! It earned Sabri Kouki first prize in a seafood recipe competition. In Arabic, this tagine is called *Tej el Molk*, which literally means the crown of royalty. The large shrimp decorating the dish come from the Tunisian coastal region, and these gems are placed on top of the golden tiara.

The large shrimp turn red during cooking and resemble the species known as "bouquet" found along the French coasts. Make sure those you choose are quite bright and firm. They should have a pleasant aroma. (If you can't get shrimp, use the white flesh from cuttlefish, calamari, mussels, or a smaller variety of cuttlefish.) Reserve some shrimp for the final decoration. For the croquettes, our chef suggests that if you don't want to make a batter you can coat them with breadcrumbs instead.

In Tunisia, the tagine comes in a variety of forms, but above all it should always be browned and be made largely of eggs. It can also contain meat, fish, onions, navy beans, or cheese. There's not just one interpretation of the tagine—every Tunisian family has its own version!

Finally, to complement the flavors of the "Royal Crown Tagine," you need a tartare sauce. The base of this dressing is mayonnaise. Mix the egg yolk with a teaspoon of prepared mustard and a pinch of salt. Next, trickle sunflower oil slowly over the mixture, while continuously stirring. Then add 1 teaspoon of chopped capers and 1 teaspoon of chopped parsley. Add 1 teaspoon of chopped onion and 1 teaspoon of chopped hard-boiled egg. To thin out the sauce, add 1 teaspoon of water. It will have a smoother consistency!

Cook the raw and shelled shrimp for 2–3 minutes in boiling water. Drain and place to one side. Keep back 14 oz (400 g) shelled shrimp. Chop and mix 3¹/₂ oz (100 g) of these with 3¹/₂ tbsp (50 g) of the cheese. Mix in 1 whole egg. Season with salt and pepper. Pit and chop the olives.

Blend half the chopped olives with this shrimp mixture. Add the cumin. Set aside the remaining chopped olives. Preheat your oven to 400 °F/200 °C.

Using the palms of your hands, make small balls with the shrimp mixture. Retain half of the shrimp for decoration, and fry the rest gently for 1 min in the chopped tomato mixture with 1 tbsp (15 ml) olive oil. Then shell these shrimp.

Tagine

Make the batter by mixing the all-purpose flour, beer, salt, and egg. Leave to ferment for 30 minutes, then dip the balls in the batter. Fry the battered croquettes in the cooking oil. Keep them hot.

Beat the 10 eggs, blend in the rest of the grated Swiss cheese, chopped olives, and the reserved 14 oz (400 g) shrimp. Arrange the browned, shelled shrimp at the bottom of a savarin mold. Pour in the egg mixture. Bake in the oven for 15 minutes at 400 °F/200 °C.

Turn out the tagine. Decorate it with the unshelled shrimp and the croquettes held on firmly with cocktail sticks all around the crown. Serve warm with the tartare sauce.

Kaftaji

Preparation time:	25 minutes
Cooking time:	50 minutes
Difficulty:	★

Serves 4

8	eggs
12 oz/350 g	lamb's liver and heart
7 tbsp/100 ml	Tunisian olive oil
1 oz/30 g	chopped onion
½ tbsp/8 g	tomato paste
1 pinch	ground turmeric
5 oz/150 g	red squash

5 oz/150 g	hot green chiles
7 oz/200 g	fresh tomatoes
7 oz/200 g	potatoes
	oil for frying
1 pinch	ground coriander
3½ oz/100 g	dry bread
3 or 4 sprigs	flat-leaf parsley, chopped
¾ tbsp/10 g	unsalted butter for the mold
	salt and pepper

Originating from Kairouan, the *kaftaji tajine* is a combination of two typically Tunisian, delicious recipes. In Tunisia, gourmets call a *tajine* a dish consisting of a meat, vegetable, or fish filling, flavored with onions and parsley, thickened with beaten eggs and browned in the oven. However, the *kaftaji* blends hot chiles, fried and chopped tomatoes and red squash, with added salt, pepper and spices, then enriched with chopped fried eggs. Our chef mixes raw and cooked eggs in his recipe and adds fried potatoes.

Chokri Chteoui decided on a *kaftaji tajine*, a tart which incorporates small cubes of offal. Tunisians enjoy lamb or beef liver, heart, and kidneys, which are used as tasty fillings for zucchini, eggplants, and peppers. The best known specialty is the *klaya*, an assortment of offal which is browned in oil, and simmered in tomato paste or flavored with turmeric.

Instead of lamb offal, you could choose small pieces of octopus, shrimp, poultry, or beef. You can even enjoy a vegetarian *tajine kaftaji*, using vegetables such as peas, potatoes, carrots, parsley, and onion.

Our chef also recommends that having made this dish you can go further and create a *tajine malsouka*. To make this, line the mold with fritter sheets, coated with melted, unsalted butter, and arrange the filling inside. Cover with other buttered fritter sheets and brown in the oven.

In large Tunisian families, the filling for this dish is simply poured onto a plate and baked in the oven, The *tajine* is cut into rectangles or triangles, and served hot or cold. A cakepan, or individual ramekins, are also suitable receptacles for cooking this dish. A tomato sauce spiced up with garlic, harissa, and caraway seeds is generally served as an accompaniment.

Boil 2 of the eggs for 10 minutes until hard. Place them to one side. Cut the lamb's liver and heart into strips, then into small cubes. Season with salt and pepper. Preheat oven to 350 °F/180 °C.

Heat the olive oil. Add the cubes of lamb and the onion, and stir until they're browned on all sides. Blend in the tomato paste and turmeric. Add a glass of water, and allow to cook.

Cut the squash into slices then peel it. Remove the stalk and seeds from the peppers. Rinse and wipe the tomatoes. Peel the potatoes and slice them. Fry these vegetables one after the other in hot oil until golden brown.

Tagine

Dice the fried tomatoes, squash, chiles, and potatoes. Put them in a large basin. Season with coriander, salt, and pepper.

Shell, then chop the hard-boiled eggs. Grate the dry bread to make breadcrumbs. Put the cooked meat into a basin. Add the chopped eggs, breadcrumbs, and the cubes of fried vegetables.

Break 6 eggs into a bowl. Pour them into the meat and vegetable mixture. Season and add chopped parsley. Grease a round cakepan with unsalted butter. Fill with the mixture, and smooth out the surface. Brown in the oven for about 20 minutes. Turn out and divide into portions.

Souani

Preparation time:	*30 minutes*
Cooking time:	*45 minutes*
Difficulty:	✶

Serves 4

1¼ lb/500 g	eggplants
1¼ lb/500 g	zucchini
	cooking oil
8¾ oz/250 g	shoulder of lamb
1	onion, chopped
3½ tbsp/40 ml	olive oil
1 tsp	turmeric
7½ tbsp/120 g	grated cheese
8	eggs
	salt and pepper

The word *souani* can be translated as "kitchen garden," and this is a good description for Bizerte and its region. This Phoenician-founded city is primarily renowned for its shipping trade, but it is also famous for its market gardening, thanks to the Moors, who introduced it when they were driven out of Spain.

The Tunisian *tajine* is a kind of "tart," made from eggs and grated cheese which are combined with meat and various vegetables. A traditional dish from Bizerte, it is typically Mediterranean. This tagine features eggplants and zucchini cut into circles. These summer vegetables have found their niche in the culinary heritage of most of North Africa and Southern Europe.

The zucchini should be fried first as they absorb less oil than the eggplants. Originating from Central America, they have quite a high water content, but are low in calories. Our chef advises selecting the small ones, for their tender flesh. Their uniform color should be blemish-free. The stem section should be fresh and unwrinkled. Zucchini are eaten with or without the skin. Scrape the skins if you don't want to peel them.

There are many varieties of eggplants, and they are a great favorite of the Tunisians. They can be long, round, black, purple, or white. Choose eggplants with a smooth, intact skin, and if possible a very fresh stalk. Avoid those that are too large; they're often filled with seeds. Eggplants have a strong flavor and go well with tomatoes, zucchini, garlic, and olives, or, as in this recipe, with lamb.

The *tajine souani* is a real delight. You can follow Fethi Tounsi's instructions and cook it in small ramekins to make individual portions, or if you prefer a more traditional presentation, use a large dish.

Wash the eggplants and the zucchini. Cut them into circles.

Gently fry the eggplant and zucchini slices in cooking oil. Drain and absorb the excess oil on a paper towel. Season with salt and pepper.

Dice the boned shoulder of lamb.

Tagine

Brown the chopped onion in the olive oil. Add the cubes of lamb. Season with salt, pepper, and turmeric. Fry gently for 10 minutes and pour the contents into a bowl.

Add ⅓ cup (80 g) of the grated cheese and 4 of the eggs. Mix well. Break the remaining eggs into a separate bowl, and add the rest of the grated cheese, mix well, and place to one side.

Grease the ramekins. Put in a layer of the vegetable slices, then the lamb mixture. Cover with vegetable slices. Pour the egg and cheese mixture over the top. Cook in a double boiler in the oven at 350 °F/180 °C for approximately 15 minutes. Turn out. Arrange the tagine on a plate.

Tchich

Preparation time:	20 minutes		
Cooking time:	1 hour		
Difficulty:	★		

Serves 4

10¹/₂ oz/300 g	gray bream	¹/₂ tsp	harissa
1 oz/30 g	chopped onion	3 cloves/5 g	garlic, chopped
6¹/₂ tbsp/100 ml	Tunisian olive oil	¹/₂ tsp	chile powder
2	fresh tomatoes	¹/₃ cup/80 g	medium-sized *chorba frik*
1 tbsp/17 g	tomato paste	1 small piece	celery
¹/₂ tsp	ground caraway seeds	2 or 3 sprigs	flat-leaf parsley, chopped
		1	lemon, sliced
			salt and pepper

The soup known as *tchich* is a great favorite in the towns of the Sahel region and is often served during the month of Ramadan. This popular dish made from ground green wheat, chile powder, and spices has many variations on the theme. Chokri Chteoui loves making it with a mixture of small fish, as well as with gray bream, dried octopus, rock or grouper fish. Inland, *tchich* is usually served with pieces of chicken and lamb. On chilly early mornings, Tunisians sometimes warm themselves with a portion of vegetarian *tchich*, which is flavored with a generous quantity of garlic.

Tunisians are very inventive when it comes to original cereal mixtures and they sprinkle very small pieces of *chorba frik* into this soup. *Chorba frik* come from ears of wheat, which are cut before they're completely ripe, warmed between layers of straw, and then beaten. After rinsing, the grains produced are then mixed with salt, dried in the sun, sorted, ground, and finally winnowed. After sifting, which removes the bran, the remaining fragments are sieved and divided into three categories: fine grains for making bread; medium-sized grains for soups; and large grains for couscous. Like many Tunisian housewives, our chef's mother makes her own *frik* for her *tchich*. However, it is now also available ready-made.

Our chef advises you to spice up the *tchich* with bream with *dyari* harissa, which is a rather strong variety made from dried chiles, garlic, salt, and caraway seeds. But any variety of harissa will flavor your recipe.

Chokri Chteoui usually flakes the fish meat into the soup just before he serves it. You can also add the tails or large pieces of bream to decorate the dish.

Scale, gut, clean, and rinse the bream. Remove the head. Cut the body through the middle into 2 equal halves. Sprinkle salt and pepper both inside and over the skin of the fish. Place to one side.

Brown the onion in a stockpot in a little olive oil.

Skin, deseed, and chop the tomatoes. Mix the tomato paste in a little water. Add the onion, a pinch of the caraway seeds, tomato paste, harissa, chopped tomatoes, garlic, salt, pepper, and chile powder. Stir. Cook for 10 minutes.

with Bream

Pour 4 cups (1 liter) water into the mixture. Bring to the boil. Immerse the fish in the boiling stock. Season with salt, pepper, and the rest of the caraway seeds. Cover. Cook for 20–30 minutes.

When the pieces of fish are well cooked, remove them from the sauce using a skimmer. Arrange in a dish and place to one side.

Pour 2 cups (500 ml) water into the sauce. Bring to the boil. Add the chorba frik and the chopped celery. Blend and cover. Cook for 15 minutes over a medium heat. Adjust the seasoning. Serve with the fish meat, chopped parsley, and lemon slices.

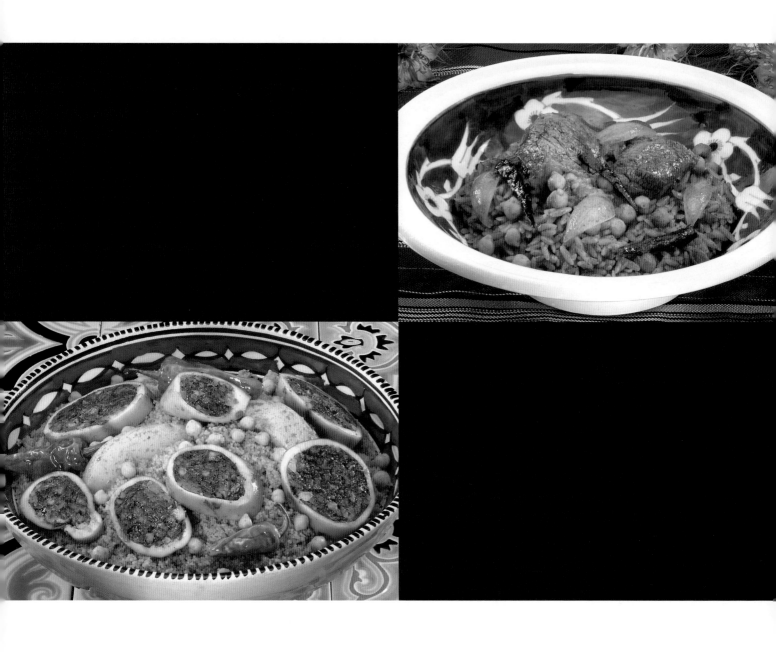

Couscous & Pasta

Preparation time:	1 hour
Cooking time:	2 hours 5 minutes
To soak the garbanzo beans:	12 hours
Difficulty:	★★

Serves 4

14 oz/400 g	octopus
3½ oz/100 g	*mhamsa* (pasta)
1¼ cups/200 g	fine semolina
1	half chicken
6½ tbsp/100 ml	olive oil
1 tbsp	harissa
1 tbsp	tomato paste
2 oz/50 g	dried sardines, soaked

¼ cup/50 g	garbanzo beans (chickpeas), soaked overnight
1 tsp	paprika
1 tsp	caraway seeds
1 tsp	ground coriander
2 tbsp/20 g	lentils
2 dried	chiles
¾ cup/150 g	small fava beans (broad beans)
4	garlic cloves
	salt and pepper

Barkoukech is a specialty, typical of the oasis at Tozeur, in the far southwestern corner of Tunisia. This dish is made to celebrate the arrival of spring. *Barkoukech* is the name of the pasta, which is kneaded by hand. Moistened with a little water, the minuscule *mhamsa*, blended with fine semolina, take the form of a peppercorn during this process. Our chef adds water only when the pasta dries between his fingers.

This popular dish is noted for combining the flavors of chicken and dried sardines. Sardines are a great favorite of Mediterranean people, and are easy to prepare. They are very plentiful in the seas near Tunisia, and can be caught in spring and summer. When salted and then dried on the sand, the sardines are known as *chilba*. Before use they are soaked in water to clean them.

Octopus should be available from your fishmonger throughout the year. It has quite delicate flesh, which must be beaten for a long time to tenderize it, and then blanched in boiling water.

The chicken makes the *barkoukech* a nourishing dish. Mimoun Arroum suggests that after the chicken is cut up, you use the carcass and the giblets in the mixture to enhance the flavor. If you can, choose a chicken raised on grain, with plump, firm, and slightly fatty meat.

A symbol of spring, small fava beans quite naturally appear in this recipe. Originating from Persia and Africa, fava beans have been eaten in the Mediterranean basin since ancient times. With young beans, there's no need to remove the delicate skin.

Under no circumstances should the *barkoukech* be reheated. Families from Tozeur enjoy this pasta-based ragout either hot or cold.

Cut the octopus into pieces and cook for 1 hour 20 minutes in water. Spread out the mhamsa in a dish and moisten with a little water. Mix with your fingers.

Sprinkle the fine semolina into the mix, and add a little water while continuing to mix with your fingertips. The small balls of pasta should be about the size of a peppercorn.

Cut up the ½ chicken and fry gently in the olive oil. Add the harissa and tomato paste. Mix well. Add the sardines, and the garbanzo beans soaked overnight.

Barkoukech

Season with paprika, caraway seeds, coriander, and salt. Add the lentils and cover with 4 cups (2 liters) water. Cook for approximately 30 minutes.

Add the whole dried chiles, small fava beans, and octopus pieces. Cook for approximately 25 minutes. Cook the mhamsa in a couscous steamer for 20 minutes.

Pour the mhamsa into the mixture. Add the crushed garlic cloves. Season with pepper. Cook for 15 minutes. Arrange the barkoukech on a dish, topping the mhamsa with the chicken, octopus, and sardines.

Borghol

Preparation time:	20 minutes
Cooking time:	55 minutes
To soak the	
garbanzo beans:	12 hours
Difficulty:	★

Serves 4

1¼ lb/500 g	shoulder of lamb
6 tsp/30 g	ground turmeric
3½ tbsp/50 g	ground paprika
4	garlic cloves, crushed
7 tbsp/100 ml	Tunisian olive oil
2	onions, thinly sliced

4 tsp/20 g	tomato paste
¼ cup/50 g	garbanzo beans (chickpeas), soaked overnight
1½ cups/300 g	large bulgur wheat
¼ cup/70 g	fresh peas
	salt and black pepper

For the decoration:

4	green mild or hot chiles, fried

A very popular dish, the *borghol bil allouche* is a great favorite throughout Tunisia. It is very similar in appearance and flavor to lamb risotto, but with one crucial difference—locally produced *borghol* is cooked with the lamb instead of rice, which has to be imported.

Made from blanched wheat, *borghol* is widely eaten in Tunisia. The fertile plain of Mateur, in the north, as well as the governorships of Jendouba and Béja in the northwest, produce most of the country's cereals. After an initial grading, the grains of wheat are cooked in boiling salted water, then drained and dried in the sun. Next, they are ground in a mortar, or crushed in the village mill. Finally, the grain is sieved. Nowadays, these complex preparations are increasingly carried out on an industrial basis.

Fine *borghol* is used to make delicious soups, while the larger-grained version is cooked in a meat sauce and served as a main course. *Borghol* is also frequently served as part of a salad, where it is mixed with tomatoes, olive oil, salt, and pepper, and many Tunisians eat it for breakfast, sprinkled with milk and liquid honey.

Cooking *borghol* is similar to cooking rice for a risotto: allow two volumes of water to one volume of cereal. Following a method passed down from his grandmother, Mohamed Boussabeh adds water to the spices that remain at the bottom of the dish in which he has coated the meat. Then he pours this flavored liquid into the *borghol*, which is much better than simply adding a glass of water!

Also, our chef advises that cooking a few lamb bones with the meat will strengthen the flavor of the dish. Of course, the same recipe can be produced with pieces of rabbit or free-range chicken.

Bone the shoulder of lamb. Cut up the meat into large cubes of approximately 1¾ oz (50 g) and place in a large dish.

Sprinkle salt, pepper, turmeric, paprika, and ground garlic over the meat. Sprinkle olive oil liberally over the mixture. Turn the meat thoroughly with your hands so that the meat is well covered with the spices.

Pour a trickle of olive oil into a stockpot, add the onion slices, tomato paste, spicy lamb pieces, and the garbanzo beans.

Bil Allouche

Pour approximately 2 glasses of water into the saucepan. Bring to the boil.

When the mixture has come to the boil, add the borghol. Stir well and cover. Cook for approximately 35 minutes. Stir occasionally during cooking.

Finally, add the fresh peas. Stir in. Pour the contents into a gratin dish and finish cooking under the oven broiler for 10 minutes. Decorate with fried green mild or hot chiles.

Steamed Chorba

Preparation time:	*20 minutes*
Cooking time:	*1 hour 15 minutes*
Difficulty:	★★

Serves 4

2¹/₂ lb/1 kg 200g	leg of lamb
4 tbsp/60 ml	olive oil
1 large	onion, thinly sliced
2 tbsp/35 g	tomato paste
1 tsp	harissa

2	carrots
2	potatoes
2	green bell peppers
2¹/₂ cups/500 g	*chorba* or large "*langues d'oiseaux*" ("birds' tongues"— short pasta)
	allspice
	salt and pepper

Chorba m'faoura is a Tunisian culinary classic. Translated as "steamed chorba with lamb," it's often served at family gatherings. The short variety of pasta, shaped like grains of rice, which makes this hearty dish, is called *chorba*, or more poetically "*langues d'oiseaux*" ("birds' tongues").

This minuscule variety of pasta is a legacy of the Italians, but it has become a common feature of Tunisian cuisine. The pasta, made from durum wheat flour, is rolled and very carefully kneaded between the fingers. This process, requiring the dexterity of a clockmaker, is industrialized nowadays, much to the relief of busy cooks! It is widely available and can be bought in several sizes. The smallest variety cooks very quickly.

In the past in Tunisia, this lamb dish would cook slowly over the charcoal of the traditional *kanoun*—a terracotta brasero—which was used in every household. If you are unable to get lamb, it can be substituted with veal or chicken. Make sure that you always cut the meat into small pieces; Tunisian families have a keen sense of sharing!

Lovers of strong flavors will probably want to increase the amount of harissa, but don't be tempted to overdo it as you will mask the other flavors. Garbanzo beans can be among the vegetables served with the *chorba*, which will give body to the dish. Garbanzo beans will cook in the meat sauce. Remember to soak them overnight, as they'll cook quicker. To save time with the preparation, you can buy them pre-cooked in cans.

The allspice should be added halfway through the cooking and not right at the beginning. If it is cooked for too long, it can give the dish a sharp flavor.

Cut the meat into 2 in (5 cm) pieces and cook gently in the lower part of the couscous steamer with 4 tsp (20 ml) of the olive oil, the onion slices, harissa, and tomato paste.

Cover the meat with water. Cook gently for 30 minutes. Season with salt and pepper, and a pinch of allspice.

Peel the carrots and potatoes. After the 30 minutes, add the carrots, then the potatoes, and the bell peppers. Finish cooking over a low heat.

with Lamb

Coat the pasta in the remaining olive oil in a container. All the pasta must be well coated with oil.

Put the pasta into the couscous steamer basket 15 minutes before the meat has cooked. After 10 minutes, trickle several drops of water over the pasta.

When the pasta has cooked, separate the grains thoroughly using your hands. Transfer the pasta onto the serving dish. Pour the meat sauce over the pasta. Cover with tinfoil and let it soak up the sauce. Arrange the meat and vegetables over the pasta. Serve hot.

Couscous with Chicken

Preparation time:	50 minutes
Cooking time:	1 hour 20 minutes
To soak the beans:	12 hours
Difficulty:	☆

Serves 4

4	baby artichokes
7 oz/200 g each of	zucchini, carrots, potatoes, squash
½ cup/100 g	garbanzo beans (chickpeas)
1	half chicken
	salt and pepper
1 tsp	caraway seeds
1 tsp	paprika (optional)

2½ cups/500 g	medium-sized semolina
⅔ cup/150 ml	olive oil

1	onion, sliced
2½ tbsp/50 g	tomato paste
1 pinch	saffron strands
4	mild green chiles
1	red chile

For the meatballs:

1¼ lb/ 550 g	ground beef
6½ tbsp/100 g	grated Swiss cheese
1 tsp	dried mint
6½ tbsp/100 g	chopped parsley
1	onion, chopped
2	garlic cloves, crushed
2	eggs
1 tsp	caraway seeds
6 tbsp/20 g	all-purpose flour
	cooking oil

Couscous with chicken and meatballs is a very convivial dish and is usually made on Sunday when the whole family gets together.

Tunisians are keen consumers of semolina, but they are careful not to allow it to soak up too much water during preparation so it will absorb the flavors of other, tastier, ingredients during cooking. Some people sprinkle a generous amount of stock over the couscous before serving, and then dry it in the oven for a few minutes.

In some families, the grains are perfumed with cloves, black peppercorns, or short sticks of cinnamon.

To make this dish, choose a free-range chicken, raised on grain. After cutting it up, our chef suggests using the bones and giblets to flavor the stock. Don't forget to remove them before serving the dish.

The meatballs can be prepared with ground beef or lamb, according to taste. They are delicious and bring their unique flavor to this typical Tunisian specialty. Highly flavored, they are a subtle blending of mint, parsley, garlic, onion, and caraway seeds.

Although this dish includes a substantial amount of meat, a significant proportion of it is made up of vegetables. Mohamed Boujelben advises soaking the artichoke hearts in lemon juice to stop them discoloring. The chiles are fried and added to the stock at the same time as the meatballs, but if you prefer a much spicier flavor, you can cook them directly in the dish. Cook for approximately ten minutes.

In some families, couscous with chicken and meatballs is served with a glass of whey. As an accompaniment, you can also offer your guests a spicy sauce to highlight the oriental origins of this dish.

Cut into the artichokes as far as the hearts and remove the chokes with a small knife. Prepare the zucchini, potatoes, and carrots. Cut up the squash. Drain the garbanzo beans and cook separately for 40 minutes.

Cut up the ½ chicken. Season with salt, pepper, 1 tsp caraway seeds, and paprika. Prepare the semolina by salting it. Add a trickle of olive oil and a little water. Mix with the palms of your hands. Cook in a couscous steamer for 15 minutes.

Gently fry the sliced onion, tomato paste, chicken, and saffron in 7 tbsp (100 ml) of the olive oil. Add hot water. Bring to the boil, then add the carrots. Ten minutes later, add the other vegetables, except the garbanzo beans. Cook for 20 minutes.

and Meatballs

Mix the semolina with the palms of your hands again. Then continue cooking in the couscous steamer for 15 minutes.
Prepare the meatball filling by mixing the ground beef, Swiss cheese, mint, parsley and onion, garlic, 1 egg, and the caraway seeds. Season with salt and pepper. Mix.

Make small meatballs out of the filling. Sprinkle a little all-purpose flour in a plate. Beat the remaining egg in a bowl. Roll the meatballs in a little flour and then dip in beaten egg. Seal them in hot cooking oil. Fry the green and red chiles.

Add the meatballs, the cooked garbanzo beans and green and red chiles to the stock. Cook for approximately 5 minutes. Pour the semolina into a dish and sprinkle it with stock. Arrange the couscous with the vegetables, chicken, and the meatballs on top.

Couscous with

Preparation time:	1 hour
Cooking time:	1 hour
To soak the garbanzo beans:	12 hours
Difficulty:	★★★

Serves 6

4 x 5 oz/150 g	calamari
2 oz/50 g	lamb's liver
3½ tbsp/50 g	rice
2 oz/50 g	chopped onion
4	garlic cloves, chopped
3½ tbsp/50 g	chopped flat-leaf parsley
3½ tbsp/50 g	chopped fresh dill

1 pinch	dry mint
6 tsp/30 g	harissa
1	egg

6 tsp/30 g	ground turmeric
1 cup/300 g	fresh spinach leaves, chopped
2½ cups/500 g	fine semolina
7 tbsp/100 ml	olive oil
2 or 3	cloves
3 tbsp/60 g	tomato paste
6 tsp/30 g	mild paprika
¼ cup/50 g	garbanzo beans (chickpeas), soaked overnight
2	potatoes
	salt and pepper

For the garnish:

4 or 5	green chiles, fried

Every region of Tunisia has its own wide range of couscous dishes. Semolina made from durum wheat, green wheat or broiled barley is steamed and served with a wide variety of accompaniments. Monastir gourmets make a couscous with the fish from the waters around this port. Inland, couscous is flavored with vegetables, pieces of rabbit, goat, or even *khadid* (dried lamb). *Mesfouf*, a couscous sweetened with liquid honey, dates, and cinnamon, is also prepared. Mohamed Boussabeh offers this recipe for seafood couscous, which is garnished with calamari stuffed with lamb, rice, and spinach.

Marine mollusks and cousins of the cuttlefish, Tunisian calamari are excellent in spring and summer. Fishermen from Kerkenah, the native island of our chef, use an entirely original method of capture. At sea, they enjoy hereditary fishing concessions, partly marked off by palm tree leaves on the land. In various places, they lay down a

drina, a conical lobster pot made of palm stems, with a kind of "funnel," which squid and fish are tempted to enter. Once they've gone through the neck of the pot, the stems close up and the mollusks are trapped.

When you stuff the calamari, the rice should be just half-cooked. Once inside the calamari "pockets," there's ample time to finish cooking it, and thus preserve its texture and flavor. Prick the stuffed calamari with a cocktail stick, to stop them bursting while cooking and to allow the sauce to be absorbed into them thoroughly.

If you haven't prepared couscous before, moistening the semolina can be a delicate operation. You need to pour a little water over it, stir with your fingers, and keep doing this until the semolina can be molded when pressed gently in your hands.

Separate the calamari pouches and tentacles (place the clean pouches to one side). Blanch the tentacles and the lamb's liver separately in salted water, and cut then into cubes. Half-cook the rice.

Reserving half of the onion and garlic, put the chopped onion, garlic, parsley, and dill in a dish. Add the rice, the dried mint, harissa, raw egg, salt, pepper, turmeric, and the chopped spinach. Mix well with your fingertips to make the stuffing.

Open a calamari pouch. Fill it with the rice stuffing. Close the end with a cocktail stick. Fill the three other pieces of calamari in the same way. Prick them in several places with a cocktail stick. Set aside.

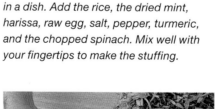

Stuffed Calamari

Pour the semolina into a bowl. Add a little cold water and a trickle of olive oil, gradually working it in with your fingertips. Finally add the cloves.

In the bottom of the couscous steamer, brown the onion and garlic you reserved. Add the tomato paste, paprika, a little water, and bring to the boil. Immerse the calamari and garbanzo beans in the sauce. Bring to the boil. Put the semolina colander on top and cook for 15 minutes.

Moisten the semolina with the cooking juice and immerse the potatoes in the sauce. Cook for a further 15 minutes. Pour the cooked semolina into a dish and sprinkle sauce over it. Cover, and leave to stand. Decorate with stuffed calamari slices and fried chiles.

Bil Meslene

Preparation time: 20 minutes
Cooking time: 45 minutes
To soak the
garbanzo beans: 12 hours
Difficulty: ★

Serves 8 to 10

2	onions, thinly sliced
7 tbsp/100 ml	olive oil
4	garlic cloves, crushed
3	tomatoes
12 tbsp/200 g	tomato paste
1	boned saddle of lamb

³/₄ cup/150 g	garbanzo beans (chickpeas), soaked overnight
3¹/₂ tbsp/50 g	harissa
1¹/₄ lb/500 g	carrots with stalks, halved
1¹/₄ lb/500 g	potatoes, peeled and halved
2	green chiles
5 cups/1 kg	fine semolina
	salt and pepper

The dish *bil meslene* couscous, usually served with a whole saddle of lamb, is peculiar to Siliana. In this north-west region of Tunisia, Bedouins have preserved the ancestral traditions. During marriage ceremonies, saddle of lamb is set aside for the guests.

Before polygamy was banned in 1958, there were stories of how wives in Siliana would compete to try to win favors from their husband. *Bil meslene* couscous became the stake in these feminine rivalries. The whole saddle of lamb was presented on the dish, and then cut up in front of the husband. Taking it in turns, the women of the harem used to carry out this ritual, intensifying the seduction.

If you want to cut up the lamb, our chef recommends browning the pieces before adding them to the vegetables. To make life easier, the saddle can be cut up before it's served on the plates.

The chiles can be fried in strips to reduce their spiciness. Chedly Azzaz suggests that you also replace pepper with cinnamon, as it has a more powerful aroma. If you wish, you can follow this example and make a *kemia* (a selection of colorful small dishes) to accompany this dish.

The success of a couscous dish depends on the preparation of the semolina. Allow approximately 1¹/₄ cups (300 ml) of hot water to 5 cups (1 kg) of semolina. Olive oil prevents the grains from sticking. To test whether the semolina is completely cooked, our chef crushes some grains between his fingers. If, on the other hand, you use semolina that is not pre-cooked, it must be steamed initially for 20 minutes, then carry out the moistening and molding process. Cook for a further 20 minutes.

In Tunisia, *bil meslene* couscous is a very substantial dish. Why not present the whole saddle of lamb as in the past…?

Sweat the onions in ¹/₃ cup (80 ml) of the olive oil in a saucepan without browning for 3 minutes. Add the crushed garlic. Mix with a wooden spatula.

Skin and deseed the tomatoes. Cut them up roughly and add them to the onion and garlic mixture, together with the tomato paste. Season with salt.

Trim the saddle of lamb. Place the whole saddle in the saucepan. Drain the garbanzo beans and add to the pan.

Couscous

Stir in the harissa. Cover the ingredients with cold water and cook for 40 minutes. Three-quarters of the way through cooking, add the carrots and potatoes. Five minutes before the end of cooking, add the chiles.

Pour the semolina into a dish. Moisten it with the remaining olive oil. Season with salt. Mix with your hand and pour 1¼ cups (300 ml) hot water into it. Allow to soak.

Rub the semolina between your palms, then pour into the couscous steamer's colander. Cook covered for 10 minutes. Remove the lid, and cook for a further 10 minutes. Add pepper to the stock. Arrange the semolina in a dish, moistening it with the stock, and cut up the meat.

Couscous with Grouper

Preparation time:	20 minutes
Cooking time:	50 minutes
To soak the garbanzo beans:	12 hours
Difficulty:	★

Serves 4

1 cup/250 ml	olive oil
1	onion, sliced
5 tbsp/100 g	tomato paste
3½ tbsp/50 g	harissa
1 level tsp	paprika
1 cup/200 g	peeled tomatoes
7 oz/200 g	potatoes, peeled
½ cup/100 g	garbanzo beans (chickpeas), soaked overnight
2½ cups/500 g	fine semolina
10½ oz/300 g	white cabbage, halved
10½ oz/300 g	zucchini, cut into sections
2	fresh onions
2	green chiles
1	red chile (optional)
1 lb/500 g	grouper fish
1 level tsp	ground cumin
1½ tbsp/20 g	salted butter
	salt and pepper

Couscous is an extremely popular dish. Some Tunisian families eat it at least once a week. Use your imagination and vary what you put with the semolina.

When many people think of Tunisian couscous they instantly associate it with fish, and this excellent specialty has gained an international reputation. In fact, depending on the region, there are many variations on the theme.

In Bizerte, in the north on the Mediterranean coast, there is an abundance of seafood, and this dish is made with large fish, generally grouper fish. Grouper is a fairly big fish, which is popular for its white, very dense flesh and rather light taste.

In this recipe the fish only takes a short time to cook, and therefore doesn't flavor the stock sufficiently. The chef suggests asking your fishmonger to clean the grouper's head. If you add the head when you start cooking the fish it will add flavor to the other ingredients, but don't forget to remove it when you serve the couscous.

A good couscous basically depends on the quality and preparation of the grain. Fethi Tounsi prefers a fine semolina. He likes to mix it, that is to say "knead" it, several times between the palms of his hands.

Although every couscous turns out differently according to the vegetables used, garbanzo beans are found in most recipes. It is important to soak them for at least twelve hours before adding them to the couscous steamer.

Couscous with grouper fish is an original, delicious dish. Like our chef, you can serve it with a small *kemia* (a collection of colorful small dishes), which will stimulate the appetite of your guests.

Pour ¾ cup (200 ml) olive oil into the cooking pot of the couscous steamer. Brown the onion slices, tomato paste, harissa, and paprika for approximately 10 minutes.

Add the peeled tomatoes, peeled potatoes, and the garbanzo beans soaked overnight.

Add 8 cups (2 liters) of water to the vegetables and bring to the boil.

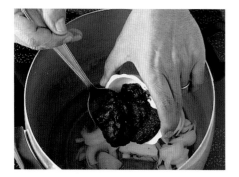

Fish from Bizerte

Add salt to the semolina and pour in the rest of the olive oil. Mix with your hands and add water. Leave to stand for approximately 5 minutes. Rub the semolina and transfer it into the colander of the couscous steamer. Cook for approximately 25 minutes and put aside.

Add the halved cabbage, the zucchini cut into sections, the fresh onions, the green chiles, and the red chile to the stock. Season the grouper steaks with salt, pepper, and cumin. Add them to the stock. Cook for approximately 15 minutes.

Incorporate the salted butter with the semolina. Mix with your hands. Starting with the fat, pour the stock over it. Arrange the couscous on plates.

Couscous with Cherkaw

Preparation time: 15 minutes
Cooking time: 1 hour
Difficulty: ★★

Serves 4

2	onions, chopped
7 tbsp/80 ml	olive oil
3½ tbsp/50 g	harissa
5 tbsp/100 g	tomato paste

4	green chiles
1½ lb/700 g	cherkaw
2½ cups/500 g	couscous
4	potatoes
7 oz/200 g	pumpkin
	salt and pepper

"Couscous with cherkaw from Monastir" is the top dish of the region. Delicious small silvery fish nicknamed *cherkaw* take center stage. The locals are so proud of them, that they celebrate them every year. A multitude of these fish appears from spring onward. Apparently, these *cherkaw* are so plentiful that the coast seems like a gigantic mirror. According to the locals, these fish are only caught around Monastir…

Cherkaw look like the small fish called smelts found in France, but they have a distinct advantage over them as they're much tastier than their French counterparts! They taste more of the sea and are very meaty. If *cherkaw* from Monastir are unavailable, in Europe you can substitute other small fish called whitebait, or indeed smelts. Usually, the heads of these small fish are removed and sometimes even their tails so that they're easy to eat. Other recipes call for the fish to remain intact, for the delight of their utter crunchiness when they're fried.

As for the stock for the couscous, it frequently consists of a very red and very spicy tomato sauce. Pumpkin is grown in the Monastir region; its very pleasant, sweet flavor tempers the fieriness of the harissa in this dish. Select a pumpkin with a very smooth skin. The seeds should still be moist. It can be kept for several days in the crisper of the refrigerator, but make sure that the pulp doesn't become too soft.

For the defining decoration, use a pastry cutter on the pumpkin. If you don't like the strong flavor of the chiles, use bell peppers instead. You can also serve the stock separately with its vegetables; and for a fiendishly hot sauce, don't forget the traditional harissa pot! You'll be enjoying a little more sunshine…

Blanch the chopped onions in 2½ tbsp (40 ml) of the olive oil. Add half the harissa, and the tomato paste. Season with salt and pepper. Add the whole chiles. Stir in 4 cups (1 liter) water.

Season the fish with salt and pepper and the rest of the harissa.

Moisten the couscous grain with ⅔ cup (150 ml) water and add the remaining olive oil. Stir well. Arrange the small fish in the bottom of the couscous steamer basket.

from Monastir

Cover the fish with the couscous grain and place the basket over the couscous steamer cooking pan. As soon as steam rises from the couscous steamer basket, allow 30 minutes' cooking time.

Peel the potatoes and the pumpkin. Cut 4 pieces of pumpkin of equal size. Cook the vegetables in the couscous steamer cooking pot by immersing them in the stock with the chiles.

Remove the fish from the couscous. Separate the couscous with a fork, pile it on the serving plate and moisten it with a little stock. Place the vegetables of your choice and small fish on the top. Serve hot. Serve the rest of the stock with its vegetables separately.

Farfoucha

Preparation time:	25 minutes
Cooking time:	40 minutes
Difficulty:	★

Serves 4

7 tbsp/100 ml	olive oil
4	fresh onions, sliced
2	tomatoes, roughly chopped
2 tbsp/35 g	tomato paste
2	garlic cloves, crushed
1 tbsp	harissa
4 dried	red chiles
1 cup/200 g	medium-sized semolina

1 tbsp	ground coriander
1 tbsp	ground caraway seeds
1¼ lb/500 g	fennel leaves salt

For the garnish:

| 1 | fennel bulb (optional) |

In Tunisia and Morocco, couscous is a popular dish. Each family has its own recipe, passed down the generations. This recipe has its origins in the Cap Bon region. Featuring fennel leaves, this vegetarian couscous turns out to have a subtle and very refreshing flavor.

The term *farfoucha* means "to mix up." In this recipe, once the fennel leaves are cooked they're mixed into the semolina. The semolina must be moistened and cooked in the couscous steamer for fifteen minutes.

Fennel, called *besbes* in Arabic, is grown in the Nabeul region. During the harvest, trucks overflow with these winter vegetables, and they perfume the roads with their aniseed aroma. For this recipe, you must use only the leaves. It's better to order them in advance from your greengrocer. If you have difficulty obtaining them, fresh dill is an adequate substitute.

The spices or condiments that flavor this dish, such as harissa, are vital and should not be substituted. Harissa is a purée made of dried and chopped red chiles, seasoned with salt, garlic, caraway seeds, and olive oil. Coriander, also called Arabic parsley, is an ingredient of many Mediterranean dishes. Caraway, which is mainly grown for its oblong, brown, and dried seeds, is an ideal spice to flavor dishes.

Farfoucha couscous is an easy dish to make. This specialty of farmers from the Nabeul region is a highly original dish and should captivate more than one gourmet!

Heat the olive oil and add the tomatoes and onions. Stir and add the tomato paste, crushed garlic cloves, and harissa. Brown for approximately 5 minutes.

Soak the red chiles in water for 5 minutes. Drain and add them to the sauce. Moisten the semolina with cold water.

Season the sauce with salt, coriander, and caraway seeds. Add a glass of water. Simmer over a low heat until the water has completely evaporated. Remove the chiles and reserve for the garnish.

Couscous

Wash the fennel leaves thoroughly and cut them into small pieces. Fill the bottom part of the couscous steamer with water, bring to the boil and steam the fennel leaves in the top part for 10–15 minutes.

Pour the semolina over the fennel leaves and continue to steam for 15 minutes. At the end of cooking, remove the lid and allow to stand.

Pour the semolina and the fennel leaves into a container and mix with two wooden spatulas. Sprinkle the sauce over them and mix well. Arrange the farfoucha couscous in a dish. Garnish with the chiles and fennel bulb (if using).

Macaroni

Preparation time:	20 minutes
Cooking time:	30 minutes
Difficulty:	★

Serves 4

2 cups/150 g	fresh peas, shelled
2	eggs
1 x 2 lb/1 kg	chicken
4 tbsp/50 ml	olive oil
1 tsp	caraway seeds
1 pinch	saffron strands

1	onion, chopped
1	garlic clove, crushed
1 tsp	harissa
10½ oz/300 g	macaroni
1	tomato, cubed
5 tsp/25 g	chopped parsley
3½ tbsp/50 g	grated Swiss cheese
	salt and black pepper

To describe macaroni au gratin, Tunisians use the term *mjamra*. In the Tunis region, recipes based on pasta are a particular favorite, and, as such, pasta may be eaten two or three times a week.

Tunisia has an excellent, sophisticated cuisine, and has made the most of the diverse Mediterranean influences. This recipe is a worthy homage to the Italian peninsula, lying just to the north. After cooking the macaroni in boiling water, it must then be mixed with the other ingredients. This tube-shaped pasta is reheated in the oven and covered with grated Swiss cheese. The cheese preserves all the smooth texture and flavor of the gratin. You can serve it straightaway in an attractive dish.

This fairly rich dish includes peas, which have been a favorite of Mediterranean people since ancient times. A wonderful spring vegetable, the pods of this kitchen garden plant are easy to shell. Select peas with a fresh green, intact, and full pod. They will keep two or three days in the refrigerator, but it is better to use them soon after you've bought them.

To give a special flavor to this dish, our chef adds saffron water to the mixture. Called *za'farân* in Arabic, this colorful spice is irreplaceable. Its distinctive flavor finds its way into many Tunisian recipes. The upper ends of the saffron are made up of the pistil or stigmas, which are dark red, velvety, and vivid.

Our chef suggests that you season the chicken with a cinnamon stick and add the carcass and giblets to the sauce.

Macaroni au gratin is a family dish that is easy to make. It's quite rich, and can be eaten at lunchtime or in the evening.

Blanch the peas in salted water for approximately 6 minutes. Drain and place to one side. Hard-boil the eggs. Shell and chop them, then place to one side.

Cut the chicken into pieces. Brown the pieces in the olive oil. Season with salt and pepper. Add the caraway seeds.

Soak the saffron in ½ glass water. Add the chopped onion, crushed garlic, and harissa. Pour in the saffron water. Stir well.

au Gratin

Cover the ingredients with water and cook with the lid on for approximately 15 minutes. Cook the macaroni separately in salted water for approximately 10 minutes. Drain. Place to one side.

Remove the chicken pieces. Cut the meat off the bone and dice it. Return the meat to the mixture.

Add the peas, chopped eggs, cubed tomatoes, and chopped parsley. Add the mixture to the macaroni in a bowl and mix well. Arrange in an ovenproof dish, and sprinkle Swiss cheese over. Broil in the oven for 5–10 minutes.

Rafik Tlatli's

Preparation time:	20 minutes		2 tbsp/35 g	tomato paste
Cooking time:	40 minutes		¹⁄₂ tsp	ground cinnamon
Difficulty:	✭✭		¹⁄₂ tsp	dried rosebuds
			10¹⁄₂ oz/300 g	cooked mussels
Serves 4			1 cup/200 g	medium-sized
				semolina
4	lamb cutlets			salt and pepper
2	chicken legs			
7 tbsp/100 ml	olive oil		**For the garnish:**	
2 slices	grouper fish, cubed			slice of lemon
8 large	shrimp			pitted black olives
3	calamari, cleaned			(optional)
	and sliced			
1	onion, thinly sliced	4	mild green chiles,	
2	garlic cloves, chopped		sliced	
3	tomatoes, cubed			

Couseïla is a fun word, created by Rafik Tlatli: "I took bits of the words 'couscous' and 'paella' to give a new name to this recipe. Actually, it's made with semolina, lamb, chicken, fish, and seafood." Living in Nabeul, this influential Tunisian chef spends time making his own creative versions of traditional dishes. With more than one string to his bow, he's also a writer, and television and radio host.

Passionately fond of his region's products, our chef only uses ingredients from the Cap Bon area, such as dried rosebuds, which are typical of the town of Nabeul.

The Tunisian coastal waters offer a huge variety of seafood. Pink shrimp with their exceptionally delicate taste are a great favorite, and bring their subtle, slightly marine flavor to the *couseïla*. The grouper is a peaceful fish found in warm seas, and is available all year round at fishmongers. Its white, very dense flesh retains its texture well during

cooking, and has a pleasantly light flavor. If you want a stronger flavor, our chef suggests that you season the grouper with lemon juice and a teaspoon of cumin before cooking it.

The mussels decorating the plates are already cooked. If you opt for fresh ones, be especially choosy when you select them: they must be completely closed and not dried out. Discard mussels with broken or half-open shells.

Semolina replaces the traditional rice in this oriental-style paella. The semolina must be moistened and then cooked in the couscous steamer for fifteen minutes, before being sprinkled with water.

Rafik Tlatli's *couseïla* is an original creation which brings the flavors and aromas of the Mediterranean region to your table.

Brown the lamb cutlets and chicken legs in the olive oil in a heavy-duty, deep frying pan for approximately 5 minutes. Place the chicken and lamb to one side.

Brown the cubed grouper fish, the shrimp, and cleaned and sliced calamari separately in the frying pan for approximately 5 minutes. Place to one side.

In the same pan, brown the sliced onion, garlic cloves, tomatoes, and the green chiles. Let them gently simmer, then add the tomato paste. Continue cooking over a low heat.

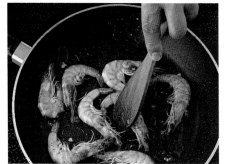

Couseïla

Pour a glass of water into the mixture and simmer for approximately 3 minutes. Return the chicken, lamb, fish, calamari, and shrimp to the pan.

Season with the salt, pepper, cinnamon, and rosebuds. Before reducing the mixture, remove the shrimp and place to one side for the garnish. Prepare the semolina by moistening it with cold water, then cook in the couscous steamer for approximately 15 minutes.

Sprinkle the semolina over the mixture. Stir well. Reheat the mussels. Serve the couseïla on a dish decorated with the shrimp, mussels, lemon slice, and black olives, if using.

Masfouf with

Preparation time:	15 minutes
Cooking time:	45 minutes
Leave the semolina to stand:	15 minutes
Difficulty:	★

Serves 4

2¹/₂ cups/500 g	fine couscous
1 tbsp/15 ml	olive oil
8 tbsp/100 g	unsalted butter
4 tbsp/30 g	sugar

1 tbsp	attar of rose oil
³/₄ cup/100 g	"Deglet Nour" dates, halved
2¹/₂ cups/150 g	white and purple grapes

This couscous, by Sabri Kouki, is a very sweet dish. The term *masfouf* is usually used in Tunisia and Algeria, meaning a sweetened couscous. It is also known in Morocco as *seffa*. The two terms refer to the generic word "grain." The difference between this sweet recipe and the salted, savory couscous is that it doesn't require any seasoned stock; it is the steam rising from the water in the couscous steamer's pan that cooks it. *Masfouf* is a dry mixture, but has a generous amount of unsalted butter. It is served during the month of Ramadan, often eaten before going to bed, accompanied by a refreshing glass of milk or tea. Occasionally, some Tunisian families even moisten it with milk and supplement it with dried fruits. Served in this way, it's a great favorite during this fasting period because of its nutritional value.

The famous Tunisian dates that top the *masfouf* with sunshine fruits, are also called *deglet nour*. In Tunisian, this name means "fingers of light," because they acquire a certain amber-colored transparency when they ripen. These dates are simply the best! They are a product of superior quality and are often sold in the shops under the label "deglet nour of Tunis." Being the only dates that can be presented attached to their stems, you'll easily recognize them.

Grapes are grown in the Cap Bon region and in the Sahel. The white and purple grapes in the recipe are extremely sweet and can also be replaced by the delicious pomegranate. *Masfouf* supplemented by this classical fruit is a very great favorite of the Tunisian middle class. The pulp from the translucent, iridescent pomegranate is a fitting accompaniment to the geranium-attar extract (rose oil), which is distilled in the Cap Bon region and flavors many pastries. This couscous is very often served as a light meal rather than as a dessert.

Moisten the couscous with cold water and cover it thoroughly. Soon after, remove the excess water from the semolina, leaving the semolina to stand for 15 minutes. Preheat the drained water in the bottom part of the couscous steamer ready to cook the semolina.

The couscous is ready when the surface crackles. Stir in 1 tbsp of olive oil and separate the grains with your fingertips. Roll it between your hands and crumble all the small lumps, removing any that do not crumble.

Put the semolina into the couscous steamer and cook it for 20 minutes. Take it off the heat; if it seems dry, moisten it by splashing some water onto it with your fingertips.

Sunshine Fruits

As soon as the couscous is cooked and very hot, add the unsalted butter with your fingers, and the sugar. Remove the grains with the whisk and add a few drops of attar of rose oil.

Transfer the couscous to the savarin mold. Press it down thoroughly.

Turn out the masfouf and top it with halved dates. Put the green and purple grapes into the center of the crown and serve warm.

Noicer Pasta

Preparation time: 45 minutes
Cooking time: 35 minutes
To soak the
  garbanzo beans: 12 hours
Difficulty: ★★

Serves 4

1	chicken
	olive oil
5 oz/150 g	onions, chopped
4 tsp/20 g	tomato paste
1/2 cup/100 g	garbanzo beans (chickpeas), soaked overnight

3/4 cup/100 g	small peas
14 3/4 oz/450 g	*noicer* pasta
1/2 tbsp/5 g	salted butter
	ground cinnamon
	ground rosebuds
	salt and pepper

For the garnish:

4	green peppers, fried

Here Ali Matri serves a sophisticated dish, typical of Tunisian cuisine, consisting of very thin, small squares of pasta, which are steamed and flavored with cinnamon and ground rosebuds, and served with chicken in onion sauce, garbanzo beans, and peas.

Noicer pasta is made with three-quarters semolina and one-quarter all-purpose flour. When cooked, it should retain the flavor and a little of the crunchiness of the semolina. To begin with, the cook prepares noodles or *rechta*. A very long and very delicate rolling pin is used to roll it out as thinly as possible. Next it is cut into strips and then into small squares, which are dried on sieves. In Tunisia, *noicer* pasta is still homemade. You could possibly use thin fresh lasagne sheets instead, which you then cut into squares.

Noicer pasta is always steamed and never cooked in boiling water. In contrast to the couscous semolina, it is cooked just the once in the couscous steamer. Then it is tipped onto a dish, the cooked meat juices are drizzled over, it is covered and cooked over a very low heat until all the sauce has been thoroughly absorbed.

Because the uncooked pasta is coated with olive oil, to stop it from sticking when it is steamed, Ali Matri is careful to cook the chicken in only a very small amount of olive oil. That way, when the pasta is mixed with the chicken sauce, it isn't too greasy. He sometimes makes this recipe with lamb instead of chicken.

To season his *noicer* pasta, Ali Matri recommends the same combination of flavors as in the couscous: two-thirds cinnamon and one-third ground rosebuds. He prepares this delicious mixture from freshly bought spices, and uses it to sprinkle over a large number of dishes, including his pastries.

Gut and clean the chicken. Remove the legs. Cut the chicken in half through the belly and cut the whole chicken into 8 portions. Sprinkle salt and pepper over the pieces.

Pour 3 1/2 tbsp (50 ml) olive oil into the bottom part of the couscous steamer, and then add the seasoned pieces of chicken.

Sprinkle the chopped onions over the chicken. Add the tomato paste and half a glass of water. Simmer for a few moments, then cover with water up to the level of the chicken. Add the drained garbanzo beans and the peas. Bring to the boil. Cook for 10 minutes.

with Chicken and Peas

Pour the noicer pasta into a dish. Trickle some olive oil over it, while mixing with your fingertips to thoroughly soak the pasta with the oil.

When the chicken has cooked for 10 minutes, place the colander on the base of the couscous steamer. Pour some of the pasta into the colander. Bring to the boil. When the steam rises, add the rest of the pasta. Cook the chicken and pasta for 1 minute, then pour the pasta into a dish.

Add salted butter, cinnamon, and ground rosebuds to the pasta. Pour a ladletul of cooked chicken stock over the mixture. Cover. Cook the pasta until it has absorbed the stock. Serve with the chicken and sauce, and garnish with fried green peppers.

Tlitlou

Preparation time:	*2 hours 20 minutes*
Cooking time:	*1 hour*
To dry the tlitlou:	*12 hours*
To soak the	
garbanzo beans:	*12 hours*
Difficulty:	★★

Serves 4

1¼ oz/600 g	shoulder of lamb
1	dry hot red pepper
¾ cup/200 ml	olive oil
2	onions, 1 thinly sliced
1 tbsp	harissa
1 tsp	paprika

2 tbsp/35 g	tomato paste
½ cup/100 g	garbanzo beans (chickpeas)
1½ tbsp/20 g	salted butter pepper

For the *tlitlou*:

2½ cups/500 g	fine semolina
1 tsp	yeast (if using active dry yeast, follow maker's instructions)
1	trickle olive oil salt

Tlitlou is another variety of small pasta, made with semolina, yeast, salt, olive oil, and water. It is handmade and requires patience. This specialty of the Bizerte region is mainly prepared for the Muslim feast of *Aïd el Kebir*, the day when a lamb is sacrificed. On the eve of the feast, women set to work and make these small pieces of pasta, the size of a grain of rice. Then they dry them on a sieve overnight and prepare this traditional dish for dinner. If you are short of time, you can always use "langues d'oiseaux" or short macaroni instead of *tlitlou*.

Lamb is an essential ingredient of this dish; it is tender, aromatic, and full of flavor. Either use shoulder of lamb, as the chef has done here, or use neck of lamb instead.

Subtly spiced, this dish stimulates the taste buds. Harissa, which is used as a condiment in Tunisian cooking, is a purée of dried red chiles, chopped and seasoned with salt, garlic, caraway seeds, and olive oil. Paprika is also often used to flavor ragouts, dishes with sauces, and even soups. In powder form, this variety of mild chile brings its distinctive flavor to this recipe.

Garbanzo beans, which are a great favorite of the Tunisians, accompany the *tlitlou*. These dried pulses, originating from the Mediterranean region, are rounded, dented, and beige-colored. They are prepared in the same way as other pulses and have the advantage of not disintegrating during cooking. However, don't forget to soak them for at least 12 hours before use.

This recipe is a legacy of the Arab-Andalucians, who settled in Bizerte at the end of the 15th century. Nowadays, Tunisian women have little time to spare with the pressures of modern life. Although many families still eat this traditional dish, the *tlitlou* pasta is increasingly rarely homemade.

Make the tlitlou *the day before, by pouring the semolina, yeast, pinch of salt, and 2 cups (500 ml) of hot water into a large container. Blend with your hands and leave the mixture to stand for 15–30 minutes.*

Make the tlitlou *into small balls and spread them in the palms of your hands. Mold them into an oblong shape, then pinch to the size of a grain of rice with your thumb. Dry the* tlitlou *on a sieve overnight. Trickle some olive oil over the pasta.*

Cut the shoulder of lamb into pieces. Season with salt and pepper. Soak the hot red pepper in water for 5 minutes.

Heat the olive oil in the cooking pot of the couscous steamer. Add the sliced onion and the pieces of lamb.

Add the harissa, hot red pepper, paprika, tomato paste, and the drained garbanzo beans. Add 1 tbsp hot water. Season with salt. Put the tlitlou into the colander of the couscous steamer. Cook for about 50 minutes, and add the other whole onion half-way through cooking.

Put the tlitlou onto a dish and add the salted butter. Pour the stock over and bake in the oven at 350 °F/180 °C for about 5 minutes. Arrange the tlitlou and the meat on a dish. Cut the whole onion into small strips and add together with the chile and the garbanzo beans.

Fish &
Seafood

Bouri from the

Preparation time:	25 minutes
Cooking time:	25 minutes
Difficulty:	★

Serves 4

2¼ lb/1 kg	mullet
⅔ cup/150 ml	olive oil
1 tsp	cumin
1 tsp	turmeric
1	onion, sliced
1¾ lb/750 g	potatoes

2	tomatoes
2	mild green chiles
1 pinch	saffron strands
1½ tbsp/20 g	salted butter
1	lemon, cut into slices
	salt and pepper

For the garnish:

| | parsley (optional) |

The old port of Bizerte, in the north of Tunisia, is as popular as ever, with its outdoor cafés where locals come to enjoy a mint tea and to admire the small, brightly colored fishing boats, aboard which the fishermen prepare their nets.

One of the most popular fish is probably the mullet. Called *bouri*, it is renowned for tasting strongly of the sea and for its firm flesh. When you go to your fishmonger, choose a firm specimen with brilliant scales, a plump belly, and bright eyes. If mullet is not available, our chef recommends "denti" or a pink bream instead.

The preparation of this traditional dish is typically Mediterranean. The mullet is baked in the oven at the same time as the potatoes, tomatoes, lemon slices, and onion. It is easy to make, yet delicious. According to our chef, the seasoning plays a critical part in the success of this recipe:

"In Tunisia, we have a popular saying which goes: 'don't prepare fish without cumin.' *Kamoun*, as we call it, makes all the difference. This word also appears in many songs, because it personifies a person's charm!"

The precious cumin is an aromatic plant that originally came from Turkestan, but now is found all over the Mediterranean region. With its warm, spicy, and slightly bitter flavor, there is no substitute for this major spice in Tunisian cuisine.

Saffron strands, which need to be soaked in water, are also closely associated with the preparation of fish. Tunisians mainly use turmeric for its intense orangey color.

Bouri from the Old Port is a delicious dish which is eaten throughout the year. When you serve it, we suggest that you add a touch of green by decorating it with chopped parsley.

Scale, gut, and clean the mullet. Cut the fish into steaks.

Pour the olive oil into a dish. Season the mullet steaks with the salt, pepper, cumin, and turmeric, and put them into the dish with the sliced onion.

Peel the potatoes. Slice some and leave the others whole. Wash the tomatoes, and cut them into quarters.

Old Port

Transfer the mullet steaks to an oven dish.

Add the potatoes, tomatoes, and mild chiles.

Pour some water into a bowl and add the saffron strands. Stir the mixture and pour it into the mullet dish. Add the salted butter cut into pieces, and the lemon slices. Bake in the oven at 350 °F/180 °C for 25 minutes. Arrange the fish on a dish with its parsley garnish, if using.

Stuffed Calamari

Preparation time:	30 minutes
Cooking time:	30 minutes
Difficulty:	★★

Serves 4

1³/₄ lb/800 g	calamari
¹/₂ cup/100 g	spinach
3	eggs
3¹/₂ oz/100 g	rice
¹/₂ bunch	parsley, chopped

1	large onion, chopped
4 tbsp/50 ml	olive oil
5 tbsp/100 g	tomato paste
5 tsp/25 g	harissa
4 tsp	paprika
1 tsp	ground fennel
	salt and pepper

Stuffed calamari from the Sahel region are enjoyed along the Monastir, Sfax, or Gabès coastlines throughout the year. This is not an everyday dish in Tunisia; however, it is made to celebrate great occasions.

Calamari are cousins of the cuttlefish. They suffer the false reputation of having a chewy texture, but this is only the case when they are cooked too long or not long enough.

To make this dish, choose medium-sized calamari, which are easier to stuff. According to Tunisian fishermen, the female calamari are more tender. To determine if the calamari is female, look at the shape of its mantle. The female's mantle is more rounded than the male's. The male's mantle also has a characteristic small point. If you buy small calamari with thin mantles, use a teaspoon to fill them. Admittedly, filling them is more laborious, but the flavor will be more delicate.

You can easily replace the spinach used for the stuffing with Swiss chard. Select very green, young leaves. They must be well-formed and blemish-free. Rinse thoroughly. Don't keep too long in the refrigerator as spinach must be eaten promptly. Keep it too long and it turns yellow and loses all its nutritional value.

Calamari go well with a side dish. A rice pilaf would be very suitable. Prepare it by browning a chopped onion in olive oil and add a cup of rice. As soon as the grains lose their translucence, moisten them with two cups of water. Serve the rice very hot. We suggest that you top it with the tomato sauce for the calamari.

Trim the calamari, remove the first layer of skin, and divide up their tentacles. Don't pierce the mantle. Rinse in clear water. Dice the tentacles, and season with salt and pepper.

Remove the stems of the spinach, then wash, and blanch it. Let it cool down, then drain and chop. Hard-boil 1 egg. Cool, then shell and chop. Mix it with the spinach and tentacles.

Beat the remaining 2 eggs, and add them to the spinach mixture along with the uncooked rice and chopped parsley. Mix well. Now fill the calamari with this mixture. Pack down the stuffing thoroughly.

from the Sahel Region

For the tomato sauce: brown the chopped onion in the olive oil, add the tomato paste and harissa. Season with salt and pepper. Stir in 4 cups (1 liter) water.

Carefully sew up the ends of the calamari pouches with a needle and thread. Prick them with a fork so that the stuffing cooks evenly.

Put the calamari in the tomato sauce, covering them thoroughly with the sauce. Cover the pan and cook over a low heat for 25 minutes. Season with paprika and ground fennel 15 minutes before the end of cooking. Serve hot.

Stuffed Bream

Preparation time:	30 minutes
Cooking time:	20 minutes
Difficulty:	★

Serves 4

4	bream
14 oz/400 g	potatoes, peeled
pinch	saffron strands
2 oz/50 g	veal liver
	olive oil
2 oz/50 g	onion, chopped
3½ tbsp/50 g	chopped flat-leaf parsley
1	lemon
	salt and pepper

Bream stuffed with veal liver is saved for special occasions and distinguished guests. Surprisingly, those living in the capital don't cook a great deal of fish, with the exception of mullet, which abounds in the nearby still waters. Bream and bass are the fish most commonly stuffed by Tunisians. Ali Matri enjoys serving bream stuffed with mussels and clams, or even fennel, lemon, and melted butter, to his clientele.

Tunisians are extremely fond of bream. It is a migratory fish that is commonly caught along the 800 mile (1,300 km) stretch of coastline. The people of Sfax and the Kerkenna islands eat vast quantities of it. The three species, royal, gray, and pink, are available in the markets. Medium-sized bream are ideal for stuffing, and the larger ones—up to 11 lb (5 kg)—usually end up being cut into steaks and cooked in a couscous.

When Tunisian cooks open a bream in order to stuff it, they make a single cut through the back. If they split it through the belly, the fine bones of the rib cage would hamper the neat removal of the backbone and spoil the flesh. When the backbone is removed starting with the tail, the main difficulty is with the head. You need to pull very hard to break the backbone, or cut it with the end of your scissors.

Be cautious when adding the saffron, because the delicate flavor of the bream is easily drowned by the powerful flavor of these crocus pistils. In Tunisian cuisine, which spice is added depends on the method of cooking and not on the fish selected. Thus, saffron would lose its relevance in a fried fish recipe.

Slices of potato cook in the oven alongside the fish. Make them more interesting by cutting them out with a mandoline.

Make an incision in the back of the bream, from head to tail. With the end of a knife, go along either side of the backbone, and detach the fillets gently. Pull the backbone out of the fish, cut it at the level of the head, and remove it.

With a mandoline or a zester, cut the potatoes into fluted slices. Sprinkle a pinch of saffron strands over them and place them to one side. Cut the veal liver into small cubes.

Heat a trickle of olive oil in a high-sided frying pan. Add the cubes of liver to the hot oil, and fry gently, while stirring with a spatula so that they are browned well all over.

from the Tunis Region

Open the fish into two halves. Season the inside with salt, pepper, and a few saffron strands.

Fill the inside of the bream with chopped onion, parsley, and browned cubes of liver. Close up the fish.

Arrange the stuffed bream on a baking sheet. Surround with potato slices. Sprinkle with a little water and a trickle of olive oil. Bake in the oven at 350 °F/180 °C for 10–15 minutes. Serve with lemon slices.

Fillet of Bass with Olives

Preparation time: 30 minutes
Cooking time: 30 minutes
Difficulty: ★

Serves 4

4	fillets of bass, 6¾ oz/ 190 g each
4	tomatoes
1	onion, thinly sliced
1	garlic clove, thinly sliced
7 tbsp/100 ml	olive oil
1	pickled lemon
10 tbsp/150 g	pitted green olives
½ bunch	parsley, chopped

1 tsp	harissa
½ tsp	turmeric
	salt and pepper

For the garnish:

2 sprigs	fresh mint
4 sprigs	parsley, chopped

Fillet of bass with olives and pickled lemon is a typically Mediterranean dish. Our chef's recipe originates from the Tunisian coast, which is well-stocked with fish. A favorite fish since Roman times, the bass, also called sea bass, is noted for the fine quality of its flesh, which is firm, very lean, and delicate. The Tunisians breed them in offshore fish farms and export about 550 tons (500 tonnes) a year to Italy, France, and Spain.

To make this recipe, you need some pickled lemon. The acidic, juicy pulp of this citrus fruit, noted for its high vitamin C content, is protected by a yellow, fragrant, and relatively thick skin. If you want to pickle your own lemons, wash them thoroughly and make an incision at the top in the shape of a cross. Then steep them in a mixture of water, salt, and white vinegar for about two months. Allow 7 tbsp (100 ml) of white vinegar to 4 cups (1 liter) of water.

Our chef suggests following the traditional method used by the villagers to gauge the correct amount of salt: take an egg and clean it. Then immerse it gently in a container holding 4 cups (1 liter) water. Add an amount of salt necessary to bring the shell back up to the surface. Then you'll have the ideal amount!

You can also use this steeping method to preserve green olives. In addition, our chef recommends it for blanching them to get rid of any bitterness and excess salt. You can also slice them thinly for a more attractive presentation.

Tunisia has more than 60 million olive trees, distributed over 4 million acres (1.6 million hectares). The production of olive oil, renowned all over the world, is an undeniable part of the heritage of this country, and an economic resource of primary importance.

Cut the bass into steaks with a sharp knife.

Peel the tomatoes and deseed them. Chop them into small cubes. Brown the thinly sliced onion and garlic in 2 tbsp (30 ml) of the olive oil. Add the chopped tomatoes. Season with salt. Fry gently for approximately 10 minutes.

Cut the pickled lemon into short thin strips and remove the pulp. Soak the strips in water to remove the taste of the vinegar and salt.

and Pickled Lemon

Blanch the olives by immersing them in boiling water for 10 minutes. Drain and allow them to cool.

Add the lemon strips, olives, and chopped parsley to the tomato mixture. Mix together gently. Simmer over a very low heat for 2 minutes.

Add salt and pepper to the bass steaks. Brush them with harissa, turmeric, and the remaining olive oil. Cook for 4 minutes on each side. Arrange them on plates and add the tomato mixture and olives. Garnish with mint leaves and chopped parsley.

Kabkabou

Preparation time:	*40 minutes*
Cooking time:	*35 minutes*
Difficulty:	✶

Serves 4

7 oz/200 g	tomatoes
2	onions, finely chopped
7 tbsp/100 ml	olive oil
2	garlic cloves, crushed
1 pinch	saffron strands

1 x 2 lb/1 kg	grouper fish
1 tsp	cumin
2	mild red chiles
2	mild green chiles
1	pickled lemon
1 level tsp/5 g	capers
5 tsp/25 g	pitted black olives
5 tsp/25 g	pitted green olives
	salt and pepper

In Tunisian, *kabkabou* is a culinary term meaning "simmering." This method of cooking is generally used for fish in sauce recipes. In the past, this delicious recipe was made in the homes of the affluent people of Tunis. Today, *kabkabou* has become a popular dish which is served on any occasion.

The Tunisian coast offers the people of this country a wide selection of fish. The grouper, a particular favorite because of its white, dense flesh, is generally average or large in size. Fairly inexpensive in Tunisia, this fish has quite a light flavor when it is cooked. If you have difficulty in removing the fillets, ask your fishmonger to prepare them for you. If grouper is unavailable, you can also make this dish with mullet, which the Tunisians call *bouri*.

Like harissa or chiles, the tomato is an ingredient which cannot be separated from the cuisine of this country.

Discovered by the Spanish at the time of the conquest of the New World, tomatoes were introduced to North Africa by the Arab-Andalucians.

Renowned for their extremely mild and almost sweet flavor, Tunisian tomatoes are delicious. In summer, select very ripe and firm specimens, preferably with an even color. If they still have their green stalk, check that they're fresh.

Boosted by various condiments, this tomato-based sauce gives character to the grouper. Our chef recommends that you blanch the lemon in brine, the olives and capers, all separately, to remove excess salt. Capers, from the caper shrub, are used in many recipes. The smaller they are, the more subtle the flavor and the stronger the aroma.

Kabkabou is a typically Tunisian dish. Very light and subtly seasoned, it should delight the taste buds of gourmets.

Peel and deeed the tomatoes, then reduce to a purée. Brown the finely chopped onions in 7 tbsp (100 ml) of olive oil.

Add the crushed garlic cloves and tomato purée. Season with salt and pepper. Simmer for approximately 10 minutes. Stir. Soak the saffron in ¹/₂ glass of water, then add the water to the mixture.

Remove the grouper fillets from the fish and cut into steaks. Season with the cumin, salt, and pepper.

Add the grouper steaks to the sauce. Simmer for approximately 10 minutes.

Wash and deseed the green and red chiles. Cut them into small rectangles. Add them to the mixture. Cook for approximately another 5 minutes.

Thoroughly peel the pickled lemon and cut the peel into strips. Add the lemon peel, capers, black and green olives to the mixture. Cook for a further 5 minutes. Arrange the grouper steaks and the sauce on a dish.

Fish

Preparation time:	25 minutes		2 cups/500 ml	cooking oil
Cooking time:	35 minutes			salt and pepper
Difficulty:	☆			

Serves 6

For the tomato sauce:

1	potato		1	onion, chopped
1¼ lb/500 g	whiting fillets		4	garlic cloves, chopped
1	onion, chopped		3½ tbsp/50 ml	olive oil
1 tbsp	olive oil		5 tbsp/100 g	tomato paste
½ bunch	flat-leaf parsley, chopped		6 tsp/30 g	sweet paprika
			4 or 5 sprigs	parsley, chopped
3½ tbsp/50 g	ground cumin		6 tsp/30 g	cumin
3½ tbsp/50 g	ground turmeric			
1	lemon			

Garnish:

2	eggs
¾ cup/50 g	breadcrumbs
1¼ cups/150 g	all-purpose flour

parsley leaves

As with children of all nationalities, Tunisian children don't like picking over a fish full of bones, and therefore turn their noses up at it. A long time ago, mothers devised a clever way to get them to eat it: simply mix flaked fish and potato purée, add some eggs to hold it together when it's being fried, and then make small balls from the mixture. Children thoroughly enjoy these flat *kefta* browned in oil. They're usually flavored with cumin. When Tunisians invite guests to their homes, they always serve *kefta* alongside the varied dishes, croquettes, and delights made using fritter sheets.

For this recipe, the chef has chosen whiting fillets, but *Kefta* can also be made with other fish such as large sardines.

When the fish is steamed, it remains relatively dry and the resulting filling is easy to mold into small croquettes. If you poach it, take care to drain it well before mixing it with the other filling ingredients. As you flake it, make sure you remove all the bones, both the small and large ones, and separate the flesh as delicately as possible. Your *kefta* will acquire a certain sophistication by doing this.

Two different spices, cumin and turmeric, are combined to season the *kefta*. After the harvest, cumin, coriander, caraway seeds, and fennel are dried in the sun. After that, Tunisians only grind the amount they need for their meals that week, in order to preserve the maximum flavor. If ground too far in advance, cumin loses its volatile aroma, and takes on a bitter taste that will completely change the flavor of the *kefta*. Originating from India and China, turmeric is available in the form of dried rhizomes. Often used instead of expensive saffron, turmeric gives an orangey color to food.

Peel the potato and cut into quarters. Put it on to boil. Poach the whiting fillets over a low heat for 3 minutes, or steam them.

Fry the chopped onion in the olive oil until golden brown. Sprinkle it with chopped parsley and remove from the heat. Stir with a spatula.

Flake the fish and remove all the bones. Place in a bowl, and sprinkle with onion and parsley, cumin, turmeric, salt, pepper, a squeeze of lemon, and the cooked potato. Break the eggs into the center of the mixture. Use a fork to mash it finely. Thicken it with the breadcrumbs.

Kefta

Take portions of the mixture and mold into small balls. Flatten them out with the palm of your hand.

For the sauce, brown the chopped onion and garlic in the olive oil. Add the tomato paste thinned with water, the paprika, salt, pepper, and a little water. Cook for 10 minutes. At the end of cooking, add chopped parsley and cumin.

Heat the cooking oil in a frying pan. Roll the croquettes in all-purpose flour and fry them in the oil until brown. Remove with a slotted spoon, then drain on a paper towel. Pour a circle of sauce in the center of the plates, and place the kefta croquettes on top of parsley leaves.

Stuffed Bass with Almonds

Preparation time:	30 minutes
Cooking time:	1 hour 20 minutes
Difficulty:	★★

Serves 4

For the stuffed fish:

10½ oz/300 g	rice
14 oz/400 g	medium-sized pink shrimp
1¼ cups/200 g	golden raisins
2	onions, chopped
3½ tbsp/50 ml	olive oil
1 pinch	ground cumin
1¼ lb/500 g	parsley, finely chopped

½ tsp/2 g	saffron strands
1 cup/150 g	shelled almonds
6 tsp/30 g	crushed garlic
4 x 14 oz/400 g	bass
	salt and pepper

For the court-bouillon:

1	carrot
1	onion
1 or 2	cloves
2 or 3	sprigs parsley
1	celery stick
1	bay leaf
1	pinch saffron
3½ tbsp/50 ml	olive oil

Stuffed bass with almonds and golden raisins takes its inspiration from a traditional Jewish recipe. But in order to be kosher (adhere to the Jewish religion food law), originally there were no shrimp, mussels, or other seafood included in the stuffing. Usually created for celebrations and ceremonies, this dish is quite tricky to prepare. You need to remove the backbone from the bass without damaging the flesh, and keep the fish intact so it can be stuffed. Pass the blade of a fillet of sole knife under the backbone, prizing it loose as you go along as far as the head, where you sever it with scissors.

Considered to be a noble fish, bass is as famous as bream, sole, and grouper along the Tunisian coastline. Officially, the sea perch fished in the Mediterranean is referred to as bass. This voracious predator, usually found in choppy waters and around rocks, belongs to the serranid family.

It has lean, delicate, and very firm flesh that doesn't fall apart during cooking, and doesn't have very many bones.

Moez Ksouda varies the stuffing by adding pink shrimp to it. The markets of Sfax and Kelibia offer "Tunisian tiger shrimp" and "large shrimp," which are both suitable fillings for the bass. If the stuffing is a little dry, moisten it with a beaten egg. When you cook it in the stock, instead of putting the fish on tinfoil, you can also close the fish over the stuffing and wrap it up like a parcel.

Almonds give a nutty flavor and a crunchy texture to the stuffing. Tunisian almond trees supply more than 55,000 tons (50,000 tonnes) of nuts annually! Harvested in May and June, green almonds are dried so that they keep all year. Available in many varieties, they grow in orchards near Sfax, Kairouan, Mahdia, Kasserine, and Sidi Bou Zid.

Put the rice on to boil for 20 minutes. Drain it. Cut the shrimp into two lengthwise (reserve one or two whole ones for the garnish). Cut the rest into small cubes. Rehydrate the golden raisins in a small bowl of tepid water.

Sweat the chopped onions in the frying pan in the olive oil. Season with salt and pepper, and sprinkle with cumin. Add the chopped parsley and pieces of shrimp (place some to one side for the garnish). Mix together, then stir in the cooked rice and saffron.

Finally, add the almonds, golden raisins, and crushed garlic to this stuffing. Simmer over the heat, while stirring constantly. Transfer this stuffing to a terrine.

and Golden Raisins

Split each fish along its back. Pass the knife under the backbone to prize it loose, cut the bone with scissors at the level of the head, and remove the bone (keeping the head). Open up each fish, and fill the inside with stuffing.

Arrange each fish on a sheet of tinfoil. Gently fold up the edges. Sweat the carrot, 1 onion pierced with cloves, parsley, celery, bay leaf, and saffron in 3½ tbsp (50 ml) oil. Add the bones. Brown, add water, bring to the boil, and reduce the mixture by half.

Add more water, reduce for 30 minutes, then filter and pour into an oven dish. Put the fish in its foil into this stock. Bake in the oven at 350 °F/180 °C for 10 minutes. Arrange the fish in the center of the dish, surrounded by the reduced sauce and garnished with shrimp.

Malthout

Preparation time:	25 minutes
To cook the garbanzo beans:	50 minutes
To cook malthout with grouper fish:	1 hour 35 minutes
To soak the garbanzo beans:	12 hours
Difficulty:	★★

Serves 4

1¼ cups/200 g	garbanzo beans (chickpeas)
10½ oz/300 g	onions, chopped
7 tbsp/100 ml	olive oil

2 oz/50 g	garlic
1 tsp	ground cumin
2 pinches	ground paprika
12 tbsp/200 g	tomato paste
2 lb/1 kg	grouper fish
1 pinch	ground turmeric
7 oz/200 g	mild green chiles
2½ cups/500 g	malthout (broiled barley)
14 oz/400 g	potatoes
14 oz/400 g	pumpkin
7 oz/200 g	zucchini
	salt and pepper

Moez Ksouda's mother has passed this recipe down to her son. She cooks the fish in a *taklia* sauce, which is peculiar to this region: a blend of tomato paste, onions, and spices browned in olive oil, reduced and then simmered with salted mild chiles, which flavor the sauce.

Made with barley, *malthout* is one of the numerous types of Tunisian cereal. Unrefined barley is sorted, broiled, and then pounded to remove the husk. It is then winnowed and ground in a mill. Through several sieving operations, the large grains called *malthout* are initially collected, next the medium-sized grains or *chicha*, and finally the flour. The *malthout* is steamed, the *chicha* is used in soups, and the flour is used to prepare the barley bread made in Sfax.

In the Tunisian countryside, the treatment of durum wheat, barley, and sorghum takes place once a year after the harvests: this is the *Aoula* season. Green barley is turned into the *chorba frik*; the ripe grains are crushed to make *asmar* couscous, or broiled to obtain *malthout*.

Tunisians can choose between red or white grouper fish. Our chef's advice is to use white grouper, which has a more tender flesh. Very plentiful, but a little expensive, this large fish is considered noble and is served to welcome guests. To spice up the flavor of the sauce, moisten the paprika, tomatoes, salt, pepper, and cumin mixture, and then add the fish head and bones and cook gently for 30 minutes. Filter the sauce by passing it through a small conical strainer.

Rinse the chiles, then make an incision 1 in (2–3 cm) in length above the stalk; salt is placed on the tip of a knife and inserted into the incision. When they've cooked in the sauce, don't forget to remove them, before cooking the grouper. Serve the sauce and chiles separately.

Boil the garbanzo beans for 50 minutes. Sweat the chopped onions in 3½ tbsp (50 ml) hot olive oil in the bottom part of the couscous steamer. In a mortar, pound the garlic with 1 pinch cumin, and add to the onions. Brown over a high heat. Add a little cold water.

Stir in the paprika, tomato paste, salt, pepper, and a pinch of cumin. Moisten slightly, then reduce this tomato sauce for 15 minutes over a low heat.

Cut fillets from the fish and remove the skin. Cut into steaks 4 in (10 cm) long. Season with turmeric, paprika, salt, pepper, and cumin.

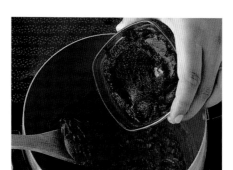

with Grouper Fish

Cut off the stalks of the chiles. Make an incision above the stalk, put some salt on the tip of the knife, and insert the salt into the chiles. Add them to the reduced tomato sauce. Reduce again over a low heat until the chiles are cooked, then set aside.

Rinse the malthout. Mix thoroughly with the remaining olive oil. Pour it into the couscous steamer's colander. Put it all on top of the tomato sauce cooking pot. Cook for 10 minutes.

Immerse the grouper fish steaks into the sauce. Cook for 20 minutes. Remove the fish, and set aside. Cook the potatoes in the sauce for 10 minutes, then 20 minutes more with the pumpkin and zucchini. Serve the fish on top of the malthout, surrounded by the vegetables and beans.

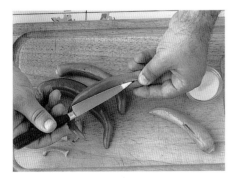

Stuffed Sardines

Preparation time:	*35 minutes*
Cooking time:	*35 minutes*
Difficulty:	★★

Serves 4

For the stuffed sardines:

1	whiting fillet
1	cod fillet
2 oz/50 g	onion, chopped
1	clove garlic, chopped
7 tbsp/100 ml	olive oil
1 pinch	ground cumin
1 pinch	ground chile powder
1 bunch	flat-leaf parsley, chopped
1 pinch	ground coriander
1/4 cup/20 g	breadcrumbs
2 or 3	eggs

12	large sardines
	salt and pepper

For the tomato sauce:

12 oz/350 g	fresh tomatoes
7 tbsp/100 ml	olive oil
1/2 tsp	caraway seeds
1/2 tbsp/8 g	tomato paste
1/2 tsp	harissa
2 cloves	garlic, thinly sliced
	salt and pepper

For the fried vegetables:

4	potatoes
4	red and green chiles
	cooking oil

Gourmets in the Sousse region enjoy creating fillings for large, very plump sardines. The third largest town in Tunisia, Sousse is one of the 40 or so ports in the country, and among the dozen which are equipped to fish at sea. Similar to Mahdia, Sfax, and Gabès, it is renowned for its blue fish, sardines, mackerel, anchovies, and bonito. For about a century, a large quantity of sardines has been caught at night by lamplight, using a very powerful lamp pointed at the waves to attract the fish.

From May until August, Tunisian waters abound in the most delicious sardines. Tunisians buy them as soon as the boat arrives at the quay, to ensure their freshness. They are cooked as quickly as possible—either broiled, fried, cooked in the couscous steamer, or baked in the oven, together with chiles, fresh tomatoes, garlic, onion, and turmeric. The port of Mahdia has important canning factories that pack the little silvery fish in olive oil, vegetable oil, or tomato sauce.

In his recipe, Chokri Chteoui prepares the sardine stuffing from a mixture of small fish, anchovies, mackerel, or whiting. But you could simply stuff them with a mixture of onions, garlic, parsley, breadcrumbs, eggs, and spices.

These sardines can be fried or baked in the oven. If you find the method of filling the sardines too fiddly, open them up through the belly and fill them with stuffing. If you can't buy sardines large enough to stuff, cut them open instead, spread an open sardine on its back and top its flesh with the stuffing. Cover it with another open sardine, placed in the opposite direction from the first. Then all you need to do is fry these small fish "sandwiches" in a pan.

Poach the whiting and cod in salted water for 10 minutes. Chop the flesh. Brown the onion and garlic in 3 1/2 tbsp (50 ml) of the olive oil. Remove from the heat and add the fish, cumin, ground chile pepper, chopped parsley, coriander, breadcrumbs, eggs, salt, and pepper.

Cut the heads off the sardines. Make an incision towards the end of the tail. Massage the sardine along its backbone to loosen it, then pull the tail gently until you can remove the backbone. Fill each sardine with stuffing, pushing it gently in with a spoon handle.

Heat the rest of the oil in the bottom of a large frying pan. Transfer the stuffed sardines to the hot oil and brown on both sides, turning them carefully. Put them to one side on a paper towel.

Sousse-Style

Prepare the sauce: peel and deseed the tomatoes. Cut into small cubes, then pass through a vegetable mill. Peel the potatoes and cut into slices.

Heat the oil in a frying pan. Using a slotted spoon, immerse the chiles in the hot oil. Allow them to brown, then drain on a paper towel. Next fry the potato slices.

In a saucepan, blend the tomato purée with the olive oil. Add caraway seeds, salt, pepper, tomato paste, harissa, and thinly sliced garlic. Simmer for 10 minutes. Arrange 3 sardines, some tomato sauce, and strips of fried chile on each plate.

Soubia

Preparation time: 20 minutes
Cooking time: 50 minutes
Difficulty: ★

Serves 4

2 lb/1 kg	cuttlefish pouches
7 tbsp/100 ml	olive oil
3	onions, thinly sliced
4	garlic cloves, crushed
4 tsp/20 g	sweet paprika
3 tsp/15 g	ground turmeric
2½ tbsp/50 g	tomato paste

1	green bell pepper or green chile
2½ cups/200 g	shelled fresh peas
2 tsp/10 g	ground cumin
3½ tbsp/50 g	chopped flat-leaf parsley
	salt and pepper

In this springtime dish, the white flesh from the cuttlefish called *soubia* is mixed with peas or *jelbana*, making a perfect combination of flavors. Peas are plentiful in Tunisian markets in March, which is when many very tender, good-sized cuttlefish visit coastal waters. In Kerkenah, the island where our chef was born, they're caught in conical lobster pots made of palm stems called *drina*.

Tunisians tend to buy cuttlefish whole: the pouches are cooked slowly in recipes such as this one, and the tentacles are used to enrich soups. First, the head and tentacles are cut off, then the body is stripped of its delicate, mauvish skin. Lastly, the cuttlebone is removed and the pouches or "whites" are cleaned.

You can flavor the water you use for poaching the cuttlefish pouches with lemon slices. Our chef doesn't brown the spices in the oil at the same time as the fish, as they would burn and turn bitter. He adds them when the ingredients are already browned.

To reduce its sharpness a little, Mohamed Boussabeh fries the cuttlefish gently in the tomato paste before adding water. Then the pouches are simmered gently, so that the sauce thoroughly absorbs their flavor.

You can add potatoes or chopped fresh tomatoes to the mixture. These will bring out the flavor of the tomato paste. Tomato paste has been made locally since the beginning of the 20th century, and is used in a vast number of Tunisian recipes. Currently, tomatoes are grown in open fields or in greenhouses powered by geothermal energy at Nabeul (Cap Bon), and in the south of Tunisia in Gabès, Tozeur, and Kebili.

Bring a saucepan of water to the boil. Immerse the cuttlefish pouches in the boiling water and poach them for approximately 5 minutes.

Cut up the cuttlefish into regular pieces, for example into diamond shapes.

Pour a trickle of olive oil into a saucepan. Add the onions, garlic, and cuttlefish. Brown the ingredients. Sprinkle with paprika and turmeric. Toss rapidly over the heat.

Bil Jelbana

Add the tomato paste to the cuttlefish. Season with salt and pepper. Stir over a low heat until it comes to the boil.

Add a bowl of water to the mixture. Cover, then cook gently for 25–30 minutes. While this cooks, cut the pepper into slices and remove the seeds.

When the cuttlefish is quite tender and almost cooked, add the peas, the pepper slices, cumin, and the chopped parsley to the sauce. Simmer for another 5 minutes. Adjust the seasoning. Serve hot.

Meat & Ragouts

Aknef

Preparation time: 1 hour
Cooking time: 1 hour 30 minutes
Difficulty: ★★

Serves 4

8	artichokes
juice of	1 lemon
2 lb/1 kg	leg of lamb
½ tsp	saffron
1½ oz/40 g	crushed garlic
2 oz/50 g	carrots

1 oz/30 g	celery
1 bunch	parsley
1	small onion
6½ tbsp/100 g	fresh rosemary
2½ cups/500 g	chorba "langues d'oiseaux" ("birds' tongues" — short pasta)
2 tbsp/30 ml	olive oil
1 tsp	corn starch
	salt and pepper

A Tunisian dish, *aknef* appears on the menu of one of the most important Muslim feasts called the *Aïd el Kebir*. During these festivities, associated with the Mecca pilgrimage rituals, each family kills a lamb. For one week, the animal is savored in all forms imaginable, and if possible in a different dish every day. *Aknef* is a piece of lamb steamed on a bed of rosemary, accompanied by *chorba* with saffron.

When buying the meat, select a leg, shoulder, or cut of lamb that can be cooked for a long time. Our chef prepares *aknef* with the "knuckle-joint," found at the end of the leg. It has a delicate flavor, and when it is finally presented on the plates, it looks perfect. In Tunisia, lamb comes either from local breeds ("beldi" sheep), or breeds of foreign origin ("rharbi" sheep).

Preparing the lamb with artichokes evokes the beginning of spring. The production of this vegetable is expanding within Tunisia, for the export of fresh or canned artichokes. In the country, they're served in a variety of ways: in salads, boiled to accompany lamb, and also cooked in ragouts and some couscous recipes.

"*Langues d'oiseaux*" are served separately. Based on noodles made from durum wheat semolina, they look like grains of rice which have been tapered at the ends. These *chorba lsen asfour*, as they say in Tunisia, come in two sizes: the medium-sized are usually cooked in a sauce to garnish lamb dishes, and the smaller ones are immersed in a court-bouillon with a lot of vegetables, to make soups. When you cook the "*langues d'oiseaux*," stir constantly so that the pasta doesn't stick to the bottom of the pan.

Peel the artichokes, and remove the hearts. Peel the stems, keep the heart, and place all to one side in water with lemon juice added. Bone the leg of lamb. Cut it up into large cubes, approximately 2 oz (50 g). Season with salt, pepper, saffron, and crushed garlic.

Pour some water into the bottom pan of the couscous steamer. Add a little saffron. Bring to the boil. Immerse an aromatic mix of carrot sticks, celery, parsley, and a small onion, in the boiling water.

Arrange the rosemary branches in the colander of the couscous steamer. Place the pieces of lamb on top. Put the colander over the pan filled with flavored water.

Surround the lamb with the artichoke hearts and stems you placed to one side. Cover. Steam the contents for 1 hour 15 minutes.

Filter the saffron and vegetable stock through a muslin strainer over a saucepan (keep $^3/_4$ cup (200 ml) of the juice, and put to one side). Cut the carrot from the aromatic mix into slices and put them in the saucepan.

Add the chorba, and the oil. Cook for 10 minutes over a high heat. Blend the reserved vegetable juice with the starch and reduce over the heat. Serve the meat on a bed of saffron sauce, surrounded by artichokes, and serve the chorba in a separate bowl.

Basine with Rabbit

Preparation time:	30 minutes
Cooking time:	45 minutes
Difficulty:	★★

Serves 4

For the *osbène*:

	Rabbit offal
3½ oz/100 g	rabbit meat
2 oz/50 g	onion, chopped
1 bunch	flat-leaf parsley, chopped
3½ tbsp/40 g	bulgur wheat
1 pinch	allspice
1 pinch	dried mint
1 bunch	Swiss chard

1 trickle	olive oil
	salt and pepper

For the rabbit in sauce:

2¾ lb/1.2 kg	rabbit
¾ cup/200 ml	olive oil
2 oz/50 g	chopped onion
2 small sprigs	thyme, chopped
1 tsp	harissa
1 pinch	ground coriander
1 tbsp	dried tomatoes
3 cloves	garlic, crushed
2 tbsp/35 g	tomato paste

For the basine:

18 tbsp/250 g	ground sorghum
	salt

Sorghum purée or *basine* forms the basis of this dish. The sorghum from Redjiche, a town some 3 miles (5 km) from Mahdia, on the east coast of Tunisia, is particularly well known. The *basine* resembles a dense, gray-colored potato purée. Our chef has embellished it with rabbit in tomato sauce, and parcels wrapped in Swiss chard leaves.

Also called "large millet," sorghum is a small-grained cereal, grown all over Africa. After reducing it to a grayish powder, Tunisians blend it with sugar, milk, and orange-flower water; this cream is called *sohleb* and is eaten at breakfast. *Bsissa* is another mixture, made by mixing sorghum, broiled wheat, garbanzo beans, coriander, and sugar.

When preparing the rabbit, remove all the fat, and always seal it well before adding the onion. If the onion is added at the beginning, it may well be burned before the rabbit is browned. The sauce is seasoned with North African harissa, a condiment made of fresh red chiles, steamed and crushed with garlic, caraway seeds, and salt.

The *osbène* accompany the *basine* in a very original way. Usually, cooks make a stuffing of fresh or dried lamb or beef offal. They insert this into pieces of animal gut, and sew them up. These small "andouillettes" (small sausages made from chitterlings) often accompany couscous dishes when guests are invited. In our recipe, the chef has prepared his stuffing with rabbit, thickening it with blanched wheat or *borghol*, and replaced the tripe with a Swiss chard leaf.

After wrapping the tinfoil around the *osbène*, prick it in several places with a knife. This way, the sauce will penetrate during cooking. When the rabbit is cooked, you can be sure that the *osbène*, which are well wrapped in their sheet of tinfoil, will be ready too.

For the osbène, *remove the rabbit offal and the piece of meat found on the stomach. Cut it all into very small cubes. Transfer to a bowl.*

Add the chopped onion to the cubes of meat, then the parsley, bulgur wheat, allspice, dried mint, salt and pepper to taste, and a trickle of olive oil. Blend well to form a stuffing.

Cut the Swiss chard leaves into large rectangles. Take a small ball of meat stuffing in your hand and place it in a Swiss chard leaf. Wrap the leaf around the stuffing, then wrap this package in a piece of tinfoil. Prepare the other osbène *in the same way.*

from Redjiche

Cut up the rabbit into 8 portions. Heat the olive oil in a stockpot, and turn the rabbit in the hot oil to seal it. Then add the chopped onion, salt and pepper, and brown the mixture.

Next add the chopped thyme, harissa, ground coriander, dried tomatoes, crushed garlic, and tomato paste to the rabbit. Mix well. Cook for approximately 10 minutes. Add a little water to dilute the sauce, and then add the osbène. Cook for 20–25 minutes.

Add 1 cup + 1 tbsp (250 ml) of water to the sorghum. Add salt. Cook over a medium heat for 10 minutes, while stirring briskly to form a thick purée. To serve, arrange a circle of sorghum purée, topped with an osbène and surrounded by the rabbit in its sauce on each plate.

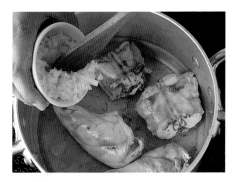

Lamb Cutlets

Preparation time:	20 minutes
Cooking time:	50 minutes
Difficulty:	★

Serves 4

2 lb/1 kg	loin of lamb
2	onions
2 branches	thyme
2 branches	rosemary
½ bunch	parsley
1 tbsp	harissa
3½ tbsp/50 ml	olive oil

4 small	potatoes
	salt and pepper

For the garnish:

	fresh rosemary

Lamb cutlets steamed with rosemary is a traditional dish enjoyed by the Tunisian middle class. In Tunisian this recipe is called *allouche fil kiskaisse*, meaning "lamb cooked in the couscous steamer."

Some families in the north-west of Tunisia add a tablespoon of tomato paste to the stock and in this way turn it into soup. Then the following day, they add *"langues d' oiseaux"* (short Tunisian pasta) to make a substantial soup.

Loin of lamb is a particularly succulent, tender part of the animal. The cutlets are delicious when steamed. When you serve the food, sprinkle the meat with its own juices. This dish must be served immediately.

In Tunisian cuisine, herbs and spices, used in a marinade, give a wonderful flavor to the meat. The climatic diversity of the country enables it to grow a substantial range of aromatic plants. You can identify rosemary by its evergreen leaves—dark green on top and whitish underneath—and its sharp flavor. You don't need very much for this recipe.

Our chef suggests you could try using fresh mint instead of rosemary and thyme. Add it to the couscous steamer colander straight away and place the meat on top.

However, don't miss out the harissa when you make this dish. This chopped, dried purée of red chiles, seasoned with salt, garlic, caraway seeds, and olive oil, is an integral part of Tunisian cuisine. It is best kept in the fridge.

Our chef wanted small potatoes to accompany this dish. This very light meal is mainly eaten in summer when the sun is at its highest.

Trim the loin of lamb and cut up the cutlets by gently breaking the knuckle bone. Place the trimmings and bones to one side to make the stock.

Remove the skins from the onions, and slice thinly.

Prepare the aromatic ingredients—chop the thyme, rosemary, and parsley.

Steamed with Rosemary

Season the meat with the aromatic ingredients. Add the sliced onions and mix. Add the harissa and olive oil. Season with salt and pepper.

Put the bones and lamb trimmings into the couscous steamer. Half fill with hot water. Add the flavored cutlets to the colander. Steam for 40–45 minutes. 15 minutes before the end of cooking, add the peeled potatoes.

Sprinkle the cooking juices over the meat. Cover the colander for approximately 5 minutes. Arrange the lamb cutlets and potatoes on the plates. Garnish with a sprig of rosemary.

Marka

Preparation time:	15 minutes
Cooking time:	1 hour
To soak the garbanzo beans:	12 hours
Difficulty:	★

Serves 4

1 cup/150 g	dried apricots
1 cup/150 g	prunes
1 cup/150 g	golden raisins
1¼ lb/500 g	shoulder of lamb
	salt
½ tsp/2 g	black peppercorns
½ tsp/2 g	ground cinnamon
¼ tsp/1 g	ground rosebuds
1 tsp	turmeric
1 pinch	cloves
7 tbsp/100 ml	olive oil
½ cup/100 g	garbanzo beans (chickpeas), soaked overnight
1 tbsp	sugar

Marka hloua means "sweet ragout" in Arabic. Of Jewish origin, this dish was prepared to celebrate Shabbat (the Jewish Sabbath), and is served hot or cold. The people of the Bizerte region have kept up this tradition and make it for marriages or for the Muslim new year.

The appearance of *marka hloua* at a meal is a guarantee of happiness. The numerous dried fruits are symbols of gentleness and benevolence.

The apricot is subtle and aromatic, and brings all its smoothness to this dish. Renowned for its vitamin content, particularly vitamin A, this round, plump, yellow-orangey fruit with its velvety skin, takes its name from the Catalan *abercoc*, itself derived from the Latin *praecoquus* meaning "early-fruiting." Tunisian apricots are exported all over the world. If dried apricots are used in this recipe, they must be rehydrated in tepid water.

This also applies to the golden raisins and prunes. These prunes are purple, and dried in the sun. However, nowadays, the fruits are more often dehydrated by immersing in a hot, sweet solution. The prune is a high-calorie food, which is rich in sugar and has a high potassium, magnesium, and calcium content. Select fruits that are very black, bright, soft, and plump.

The *marka hloua* can also be made simply with golden raisins. Select Malaga or sultana varieties. In some households, all these dried fruits are substituted with chestnuts.

Lamb goes perfectly with this sweet and slightly acidic dish. Our chef's advice is to keep the shoulder bone and to prepare a stock with celery, carrot, chopped parsley, salt, and pepper. Cook for at least 20 minutes, then pass through a sieve. Next pour it into the saucepan with the meat.

Soak the apricots, prunes, and golden raisins separately in bowls of tepid water for approximately 15 minutes.

Cut the lamb into pieces of equal size.

Season the meat with salt, pepper, cinnamon, rosebuds, turmeric, and cloves. Add the olive oil.

Hloua

Brown the meat in a saucepan for approximately 5 minutes.

Add the drained garbanzo beans. Add enough water to adequately cover everything, and cook for approximately 50 minutes. Place the meat to one side.

Add the sugar, golden raisins, prunes, and apricots to the meat juice. Cook for approximately 5 minutes. Arrange the lamb, vegetables, and fruit on a dish. Pour over the sauce.

M'Chalouat

Preparation time:	10 minutes
Cooking time:	1 hour
To steep the saffron orange- flower water:	12 hours
Difficulty:	★

Serves 4

1 pinch	saffron strands
7 tbsp/100 ml	orange-flower water
2 lb/1 kg	lamb shoulder, neck and liver
1 tbsp	turmeric
1 tbsp	sweet paprika
1	cinnamon stick
1 tsp	ground rosebuds

7 tbsp/100 ml	olive oil
1	lemon
	salt

For the garnish:

	mint sprigs
1	potato
½	lemon

Tunisians sacrifice a lamb on the Muslim feast day *Aïd el Kebir*, and the different pieces are shared out among the neighbors. The people of the Nabeul region make *m'chalouat*. This traditional dish is made of liver, heart, neck, or shoulder of lamb. It is very easy to make and is usually served at midday.

The day before this important ceremony, the women of Nabeul buy orange-flower water, which is a local specialty. The flowers from the bitter orange tree are distilled to make this preparation, used in so many Tunisian dishes. For this recipe, the orange-flower water must steep for at least 12 hours with the saffron strands, which have been broiled and then ground. This slightly reddish liquor gives the cuts of lamb a wonderful flavor.

In Arabic, saffron is called *za'farân*, derived from the word *asfar*, meaning a yellow dye, and is the most expensive spice in the world. There is no substitute for its color and very distinctive flavor.

In the culinary tradition of Tunisia, meat is always seasoned before cooking. Turmeric is a herbaceous plant, used as a spice or colorant. Curcumin is extracted from it to dye milk products, candy, drinks, and mustards. It's ground to a powder, and the root is slightly bitter. The lamb in this recipe is also flavored with rosebuds, which are another specialty of Nabeul. Dried and then reduced to powder, rosebuds are used as a spice and give a hint of sweetness to this dish.

M'chalouat is a sociable dish, usually served when friends and neighbors get together. An excuse to celebrate, it's the first hot dish eaten at midday after the long period of Ramadan. Served in deep dishes, it usually has a generous helping of sauce.

The day before, brown the saffron strands in a frying pan with no oil to give them a crunchy texture. Reduce them to powder using a pestle. Add them to the orange-flower water, and steep for 12 hours.

Cut the different pieces of lamb into portions and season with the salt, turmeric, paprika, cinnamon stick, and ground rosebuds.

Add the olive oil, and the saffron and orange-flower water.

With two wooden spoons, mix the meat in the spices until well coated. Cook the potato in salted water. Place to one side for the garnish.

Cook the meat over a high heat for 10 minutes.

Add 2 glasses of water and cook for approximately 40 minutes until you have a yellowish, smooth sauce. Before serving the meat, sprinkle it with lemon juice. Garnish with the potato and the pieces of liver, 1 mint sprig, and a slice of lemon.

Tunisian

Preparation time:	15 minutes
Cooking time:	30 minutes
Refrigeration of the olives:	10 minutes
Difficulty:	★★

Serves 4

1³/₄ lb/800 g	fillets of beef cut into 4 slices
2	pinches allspice
1 tbsp/15 ml	vinegar
5 oz/150 g	ground beef
5 oz/150 g	large green olives
2	eggs, beaten
5 tbsp/15 g	all-purpose flour
	cooking oil

1 tbsp	capers
	salt and pepper

For the tomato sauce:

2	garlic cloves, crushed
1	onion, chopped
2¹/₂ tbsp/40 ml	olive oil
1 tbsp	harissa
18 oz/500 g	can of peeled tomatoes

For the garnish:

	parsley

This Tunisian dish could just as easily have originated from Sousse or Sfax, because the famous olives grown near these towns are its star attraction. Although the vast majority of olives harvested are destined to produce the precious golden oil, some of the plumper fruits called *akhdar* are intended for direct consumption.

For a Tunisian, owning olive trees is an incalculable blessing. There are about 50 different varieties of olives in this fertile region. Olives are harvested around the month of November. When they're destined to be served for the famous *kemia* (a colorful collection of small dishes), strong flavors and often peppers can be added to them. In our recipe, the olives are blanched earlier to remove the brine and their acrid flavor.

Tunisians name their dishes according to the vegetables or the pasta used, not the meat or fish, in contrast to the European custom. In the north of the country, however, the vegetables or starchy food are often described as accompaniments.

In North African countries, meat is usually served in small amounts. The Tunisian title of the recipe says it all: *zitoune mehchi* or "stuffed olives" is a clear indication of how sparingly the locals use meat. Sabri Kouki's recipe is a sumptuous variation with the inclusion of slices of meat.

You can increase the quantity of olives and ground meat and dispense with the fillets of beef if you wish, and this would be more traditional. Don't forget the bread that goes with this dish. Buy barley bread, Italian bread, or semolina crepes to enjoy with this dish. Remember that this is a sociable dish and it's sometimes served on a single plate. Guests use their bread to carry a stuffed olive to their mouths. But first, dip your bread in the sauce. It's exquisite!

First make the tomato sauce: brown the garlic and onion in 2 tbsp (30 ml) of the olive oil, and add the harissa, and the peeled and chopped tomatoes. Cook for 10 minutes. Tenderize the slices of meat.

Add the slices of meat to the tomato sauce, and 1 pinch of the allspice. Season with salt and pepper. Add ³/₄ cup (200 ml) of water. Cover and cook gently until the oil rises to the surface. At the end of cooking, remove the pan from the heat and stir in the vinegar.

Season the ground beef with the remaining pinch allspice, salt, and pepper. Stir thoroughly to coat the meat. Set aside.

Stuffed Olives

Blanch the olives in boiling water for 2–3 minutes and drain them. Rinse in cold water, then dry on a paper towel. Cut in 2 on one side. Fill them with ground meat. Roll in the palms of your hands. Refrigerate for 10 minutes.

Cover the olives in the beaten eggs, then roll in the all-purpose flour. Allow 5–6 olives per person.

Fry the olives in very hot cooking oil. The oil must be smoking. Arrange the olives with the meat and sauce. Soak the olives in the sauce. Sprinkle the mixture with capers and garnish with parsley, then serve hot with bread.

Chicken Osbane

Preparation time:	15 minutes
Cooking time:	1 hour 30 minutes
To soak the garbanzo beans:	12 hours
Difficulty:	★★

Serves 4

1	chicken
3½ oz/100 g	chicken liver and gizzard
½ cup/200 g	Swiss chard
1 bunch	parsley
½ cup/100 g	dried garbanzo beans (chickpeas), soaked overnight

6½ tbsp/100 g	rice
1 tbsp	red chile powder
1 tbsp	chopped dried mint
1 tsp	ground fennel
1	onion, chopped
3	garlic cloves, chopped
4 tbsp/60 ml	olive oil
	salt and pepper
	mint leaves (optional)

This very tasty recipe is a specialty from Monastir. Traditionally, it's made with sheep or lamb offal, sold in portions in Tunisian butchers' shops. This assortment of meat is called *douara*. In our recipe, a whole chicken is used. If you don't want the bother of boning it, you can substitute chicken breast. If you follow this route, make the stuffing into small balls and wrap them in aluminum foil. Allow two balls per person.

Chicken osbane with rice has the sweet scent of Tunisia. It is a concentration of the flavors and fragrances peculiar to this land bathed in sunshine. The heat of Tunisia is represented by the spiciness of the small *felfel*. These strong red chiles are an ingredient of the famous harissa. On the other hand, the freshness of the dish, which should be eaten while hot, is due to the presence of the delicate dried mint, called *nàa nàa* in Tunisia. This plant pleasantly refreshes the palate and lightens the dish.

Ground fennel is easy to recognize by its hint of aniseed, a flavor which is very dear to the Mediterranean palate. This dish has a unique appearance, and differs from other delicious and mouthwatering Tunisian dishes, being so light in color. There's absolutely no tomato paste to turn it red.

However, if you want to make this chicken osbane a touch more colorful, you can make a tomato sauce, and pour some of it over a side dish of white rice. If by chance you can't get Swiss chard, use young spinach leaves instead. Mohamed Bouagga also suggests that you make this recipe with *bourghoul*, a kind of ground wheat, as a pleasant variation.

Bone the chicken and remove and keep all its skin. Remove the breast meat. Cut up the giblets and meat into small, similar sized cubes.

Wash, peel and chop the Swiss chard, and ½ bunch of the parsley. Drain the garbanzo beans.

Mix the cubed chicken meat and giblets, the chopped Swiss chard leaves, chopped parsley, uncooked rice, red chile powder, dried chopped mint, ground fennel, chopped onion, chopped garlic, and garbanzo beans. Stir well.

with Rice

Add the olive oil and mix again. Season with salt and pepper. Cut up 4 squares from the reserved chicken skin. Fill them each with a portion of the mixture. Tightly seal these balls so that all the filling is well covered.

Tie the balls with kitchen string to retain their shape.

Cook the balls in a saucepan of cold water with a sprig of mint leaves. Bring to the boil, then cover and cook over a low heat for 1 hour 30 minutes.

Lamb Ragout

Preparation time:	30 minutes
Cooking time:	45 minutes
Difficulty:	★

Serves 4

1½ lb/700 g	leg of lamb
7 oz/200 g	tomatoes
7 tbsp/100 ml	olive oil
1	onion, thinly sliced
2	garlic cloves, crushed

1 pinch	saffron strands, soaked in ½ glass water
1	lime
1	lemon
2	mild red chiles
2	mild green chiles
	salt and black pepper

For the garnish:

| | chopped parsley (optional) |

Tunisians are great consumers of lamb. It is used in many of the country's traditional dishes, where it brings its own characteristic flavor. In the Tunis region, lamb ragout with lemon is generally served as a main course. Easy to make, it is prepared all year round.

Well known for its unique jasmine, Tunisia also offers its visitors the most magnificent landscapes with rows and rows of orange and lemon trees as far as the eye can see.

Lemons have the distinctive characteristic of sharpening the flavor of food. This sour citrus fruit is liberally used to flavor soups, sauces, vegetables, ragouts, and pastries. Although some people consider it to have thirst-quenching properties, it is mainly known for its high vitamin C content. It is best to select unwaxed varieties, or wash the lemons thoroughly in hot water and rub them vigorously.

For this recipe, the lemon peel and chiles must be cut into very fine julienne strips. In the first instance, you need to cut them into regular slices of between ½ in and ¾ in (1–2 cm) thick; then stack them and slice them thinly into filaments of 1¾–2 in (3–5 cm) long.

Tunisians grow a great variety of chiles and use them as a flavoring or a vegetable. Their spicy, or even burning, flavor comes from a substance called capsine. Capsine activates the saliva glands and stimulates the digestion. They are often dried, marinated, or cooked. If you prefer a milder flavor, remove the seeds and the whitish inner membranes.

Lamb ragout with lemon is a dish full of Mediterranean flavors. Add an extra touch of color by garnishing your dish with chopped parsley.

Trim the meat off the leg and then cut the lamb into pieces. Peel, deseed, and reduce the tomatoes to a thick pulp.

Brown the pieces of lamb in the olive oil. Season with salt and pepper. Add the onion, garlic, tomato pulp, and the ½ glass of saffron water. Simmer for approximately 10 minutes. Add water until the mixture is just covered; then cover and cook for approximately 15 minutes.

Thoroughly peel the lemon and lime. Cut the peel into julienne strips.

with Lemon

Blanch the peel strips separately in boiling water for approximately 10 minutes. Drain well.

Wash the red and green chiles. Deseed them and slice into julienne strips.

Add the chile strips to the mixture. Cook for 5 minutes. Add the lemon and lime strips. Cook for a further 5 minutes. Arrange the lamb ragout with lemon on plates, garnished with chopped parsley, if using.

Okra

Preparation time:	20 minutes
Cooking time:	1 hour 20 minutes
Difficulty:	✫

Serves 4

1¼ lb/600 g	leg of lamb
3½ tbsp/50 ml	olive oil
1	onion, chopped
3	garlic cloves, crushed
1 tsp/5 g	tomato paste
1 tsp	harissa
1 tsp	paprika
1 tsp	caraway seeds
7 oz/200 g	okra
4	hot chiles
	salt and pepper

Okra ragout is a traditional Tunisian dish. It is easy to make and mainly eaten in the summer. Called *gnaouïa*, this specialty is an integral part of the culinary heritage of this country.

Okra grows profusely in the Tozeur oasis, and is nicknamed there "the Greek horn." In fact, it's an edible tropical plant and, according to species, either the leaves (Guinea sorrel) or the fruits (ketmie-gombo) are eaten. The ketmie-gombo variety is differentiated by the shape of its fruit. With ribs running the length of it, it can be oblong, short, or stocky. The ketmie-gombo is rich in calcium, phosphorus, iron, and vitamin C, and is used when it is tender, pulpy, and very green, before it ripens. Fresh okra are mainly available in delicatessens. Our chef advises only removing the stalks and rinsing the okra just before adding them to the sauce.

This is because when they are cut they release their sap, which, as it thickens, makes the okra rubbery and difficult to eat.

Although some families sometimes eat this ragout without meat, it must be perfectly seasoned. Chiles, which, together with tomatoes, were brought back from the New World by Christopher Columbus, belong to the Solanaceous family. Their spicy, or even burning, flavor comes from the capsine. This substance activates the saliva glands and stimulates the digestion. In Tunisia, the chile pepper is mainly used as a condiment. If you want a milder flavor, don't eat the seeds or the whitish inner membranes.

Okra ragout is an original dish. It is full of flavor and is a firm favorite throughout Tunisia.

Trim the meat off the leg and then cut the lamb into large pieces. Brown the meat in the olive oil. Season with salt and pepper.

Add the chopped onion and the crushed garlic cloves. Mix well.

Stir in the tomato paste and harissa.

Ragout

Stir in the paprika and caraway seeds. Mix well. Pour 3¼ cups (750 ml) water into the mixture. Cover and cook for approximately 1 hour.

Prepare the okra by cutting off the stalks.

Rinse the okra and add them to the mixture, together with the chiles. Cook for 15 minutes. Arrange the lamb and okra on the plate. Pour over the sauce. Serve the chiles in a separate ramekin.

Dar Lella

Preparation time: 45 minutes
Cooking time: 1 hour
Difficulty: ★★

Serves 4

1	rabbit
	tabil
4 tsp/20 ml	olive oil
7 oz/200 g	onions, chopped
7 oz/200 g	garlic, chopped
7 oz/200 g	fresh tomatoes, crushed

2½ tbsp/50 g	tomato paste
7 oz/200 g	potatoes
2 cups/500 ml	cooking oil
2 tsp/10 ml	red vinegar
	salt and pepper

For the garnish:

flat-leaf parsley, chopped

In the past, there was always an experienced, practical woman—be it a grandmother, elder sister, mother, or great-aunt—who ran the household in Tunisian families. This matriarch would be affectionately nicknamed "Lella" by her relations. As a tribute to his wife, our chef has christened his restaurant *Dar Lella* ("Lella's house"). Situated in Hammamet, quite close to the sea, this establishment, with its typically Tunisian architecture, opens its cupolas into the middle of an orchard of lemon and orange trees, and jasmine.

Tunisian gourmets refer to this particular ragout as *methaouma* or "dish made from garlic" in local Arabic. Ali Matri sets his own recipe apart by simmering pieces of rabbit. Cooks also make *methaouma* with chicken, veal, and even roast quail. The sauce is always identical and blends fresh tomatoes, garlic, onion, and *tabil*. At the end of cooking, a trickle of vinegar brings out the flavors of the garlic and onion. Without the vinegar, the strength of the tomatoes would mask all the other flavors.

Rabbit meat is still not eaten a great deal in Tunisia. However, the people have started to appreciate the health benefits of its meat. Also, local rabbit production is a fast-growing industry. In the countryside, wild rabbits and hares are still hunted, and there is always an abundance of them. Before simmering, Ali Matri sprinkles a very small amount of *tabil* over the rabbit. This is a mixture of coriander, caraway seeds, garlic, and dried chile powder; but while browning it may give the meat a bitter flavor. Check and adjust the seasoning later.

Potato chips are an ideal accompaniment to rabbit, and evoke memories of bygone Tunis, when storekeepers would offer thin slices of fried potatoes wrapped in a newspaper cone.

Clean the rabbit and cut off the head. Cut it into eight pieces. Season moderately with a small pinch of tabil, *salt, and pepper. Thoroughly coat the meat with the spices by rubbing them in with your hands.*

Heat the olive oil in a stockpot. Put the pieces of rabbit into the hot oil. Brown, while stirring with a spoon to avoid the meat sticking too much to the bottom of the pan.

Remove the rabbit from the stockpot. Add the garlic, onions, and crushed tomatoes, along with the tomato paste to the stockpot and sprinkle in ½ glass of water. Flavor with tabil, *according to taste. Simmer for a few moments.*

Rabbit Ragout

Return the pieces of browned rabbit to the sauce. Add enough water to cover. Cover the pan and cook for 30–45 minutes, according to the size of the rabbit.

Peel the potatoes. Cut them into very thin strips. Heat the oil in a pan, and immerse the potato strips in the hot oil until the potato chips are cooked. Remove from the oil using a slotted spoon. Drain the potato chips on a paper towel.

When the rabbit is cooked, add a trickle of vinegar to the sauce. Adjust the seasoning. Arrange the rabbit in sauce on a serving dish, sprinkle with chopped parsley, and surround with the potato chips.

Tunisian Ragout

Preparation time:	30 minutes
Cooking time:	50 minutes
Difficulty:	★★

Serves 4

2	eggs
7 oz/200 g	potatoes
1¼ lb/500 g	ground beef
3½ oz/100 g	chopped onion
2 oz/50 g	crushed garlic
3½ tbsp/50 g	chopped flat-leaf parsley
1 pinch	tabil (see below)

4 tsp/20 ml	olive oil
5 tbsp/100 g	tomato paste
½	pickled lemon, rinsed and peel cut into strips
4 tsp/20 g	capers
4	mild green peppers, cut into strips
generous 1 cup/250 ml	cooking oil
	salt and pepper

For the garnish:

| | chopped parsley |

When he prepares this typical Tunisian dish, Ali Matri makes his own *merguez*, a kind of beef meatball, molding them into the shape of calissons (lozenge-shaped candies made of marzipan). In the past, *merguez* were specifically made from lamb for the feast day of *Aïd-el-Kebir*. In our recipe, the spiced tomato sauce doesn't spoil the flavor of the beef, while it would completely mask the very subtle flavor of *merguez* made with lamb.

Ali Matri flavors his croquettes with a combination of Tunisian spices called *tabil*. During summer, cooks blend three-quarters dried coriander seeds with caraway seeds, dried garlic, paprika, or hot chile pepper. This renowned seasoning spices up beef ragouts. When it comes to kneading the *merguez*, make sure you keep hands wet so that the meat doesn't stick and the surface of the *merguez* will remain perfectly smooth.

Avoid browning the tomato paste in the oil straight away, because it will break down into noxious products and spoil the result. It is better to mix it with the *merguez* cooking juices and water.

At the end of cooking, add a few strips of pickled lemon. Any Tunisians with a lemon tree in the garden will still prepare pickled lemons in salt. The best come from winter lemons which are oblong at both ends and are very fragrant. They bring a very subtle bitter flavor to the dish, but must not cook in the sauce as they might dominate the other ingredients.

In the traditional recipe, the potatoes that accompany the dish are fried first, and then simmered in the sauce. Our chef recommends that you simply fry them instead, and then arrange them around the dish.

Hard-boil the eggs for 10 minutes. Peel the potatoes, and cut them into French fries and reserve. Mix the meat, onions, 1 oz (25 g) of the garlic, and parsley in a bowl with your fingertips.

Add salt and pepper to the meat filling. Sprinkle with tabil. *Mix well. Heat a little olive oil in a sauté pan.*

Dip your hands in cold water. Take a little filling and make the meatballs by squeezing a small amount gently in your hand to produce small, oblong merguez.

with Merguez

Seal the merguez in the hot olive oil, turning them over so that they brown on all sides. Remove from the frying pan and place to one side in a dish.

Now put the remaining chopped garlic and the tomato paste into the frying pan. Blend over a low heat, while scraping the cooking juices with a spatula. Deglaze with a glass of water. Simmer the sauce to remove the tartness of the tomatoes.

Return the merguez to the sauce. Add salt, water, and cook for 30 minutes. Finally, add the lemon strips and capers. Cook the french fries. Serve the merguez surrounded by pepper strips, egg slices, lemon strips, french fries, and garnished with chopped parsley.

Zitounia

Preparation time:	*20 minutes*
Cooking time:	*1 hour 25 minutes*
Difficulty:	✮

Serves 4

1¼ lb/600 g	boned neck of veal
2 tsp/10 g	ground coriander
3½ tbsp/50 ml	olive oil
2	onions, thinly sliced

2 tsp/10 g	sweet paprika
5 tbsp/100 g	tomato paste
2	garlic cloves, crushed
13 tbsp/200 g	green olives
1 dash	white vinegar
	salt and pepper

Olives, called *zitoun* in Tunisia, flavor this veal ragout simmered in a tomato sauce and onions. Depending on how the mood takes them, cooks prepare *zitounia* with veal, beef, chicken, or even lamb. Our chef always uses natural or stuffed green olives for the sauce, and adds them at the end of cooking. He never uses black olives, as their overwhelming flavor might spoil the taste of the sauce.

A prominent feature of the Tunisian countryside is the presence of about 60 million olive trees, distributed throughout the country. At the end of the 20th century, these trees provided 784,000 tons (711,000 tonnes) of olives annually, the majority of which was crushed to make oil. Olives ripen towards the beginning of November. The pickers vigorously shake the branches, and gather the fallen fruit on large nets placed on the ground.

Newly cut fruit are hard and sour and need to be steeped in salt to bring out their full flavor. Tunisians have developed a wide range of olive variations, any of which can be added to the *zitounia*, for example salted olives preserved in dry salt or brine, to which either harissa or red chiles is sometimes added. Alternatively you could choose stuffed varieties, filled with beef or anchovies.

When making this recipe, be careful not to add too much salt to the sauce. To a large extent, the olives themselves will provide the right amount of salt to season the dish. If you wish, you can substitute the neck of veal with a tasty shoulder. When the meat is blended with the tomatoes, add a few olive slices before adding the water and simmering, which will strengthen the flavor of the sauce.

Cut the neck of veal into large regular cubes of approximately 2 oz (50 g) on a chopping board.

Season the meat with salt and pepper. Sprinkle over the ground coriander. Turn the meat in the spice to coat.

Heat the olive oil in a frying pan, and when it is very hot brown the onion slices.

When the onions start to brown, add the spiced meat to the frying pan. Simmer for 5 minutes over the heat, until the meat has sealed on all sides.

Add the ground paprika, tomato paste, and crushed garlic to the meat. Stir over the heat, until the sauce is consistent. Add a glass of water and cover. Cook for approximately 1 hour.

During the cooking, pit the olives and cut them into slices. Add them to the ragout when the neck of veal is very tender. Stir well and cook for a further 15 minutes. Add a dash of vinegar to the sauce just before serving.

Desserts &
Pastries

Assida

Preparation time:	30 minutes
Cooking time:	30 minutes
To soak the pine nuts:	12 hours
Difficulty:	✮

Serves 6

For the pine nut cream:

5 cups/550 g	small pine nuts (from black pines)
4½ cups/500 g	all-purpose flour
2½ cups/500 g	sugar

For the white cream:

4 cups/1 liter	milk
1⅛ cup/125 g	sugar
4 tbsp/55 g	cornstarch
4	eggs
1 trickle	geranium water

For the decoration:

⅓ cup/30 g	filberts (hazelnuts)
⅓ cup/30 g	shelled pistachios
⅓ cup/30 g	almonds (optional)

In the past, *assida* cream desserts were served on feast days, in particular on the *Mouled* (birthday of the Prophet) or for the *Aïd*. The basic ingredient of the *assida* is always the same: a kind of "milk" made from pine nuts, filberts, almonds, or nuts that have been ground and soaked in water, and then filtered. Thickened with all-purpose flour or cornstarch, the "milk" is blended to a white cream and flavored with geranium-flower water or orange-flower water. The term *assida* can also be used to refer to another thicker mixture, which is similar to a choux pastry and eaten in the morning.

To make the *assida zgougou*, Mohamed Boussabeh uses very small black pine nuts. There are two types available to Tunisian cooks: the large, white, slightly oily ones, called *bondok*, that come from the pine cones of the umbrella pine; and the minuscule black ones or *zgougou*, that come from the Aleppo pine.

Our chef has chosen to dry-roast his pine nuts in a pan, which makes it easy to see how fast they are cooking. Alternatively, you can brown them in the oven. The method you use for dry-roasting has no bearing on the final flavor of the cream. Next, the pine nuts should be soaked for a long time in water, to release all their flavor and color. It is best to carry out these first two stages the day before.

When you filter the pine nut "milk," grind the mixture with the end of a whisk to get all the flavor out of it. If the cream sticks too much to the bottom of the saucepan during cooking, add a little cold water and continue beating until it is thick and consistent.

Pour this brownish cream into your goblets until they are three-quarters full; cover it with white cream, and then decorate with ground pistachios, white pine nuts, filberts, or almonds, arranged as the mood takes you.

First prepare the pine nut cream: the day before, put the pine nuts in a frying pan and dry-roast them to dry them out and improve their flavor.

Pour the pine nuts into the food processor. Add 8 cups (2 liters) water in several stages, mixing as you go along, until you have a very thin purée. Transfer to a bowl and leave to soak for 8–12 hours in a cool place.

After soaking the pine nut purée, use a small ladle to pour it into a conical strainer and filter into a large bowl.

Zgougou

Sieve the all-purpose flour and add it gradually to the liquid, beating vigorously. Add the sugar, and beat in the same way. Heat the mixture in a saucepan until it is thick like a confectioners' custard. Pour into the goblets and leave to cool.

To make the white cream, bring 3 cups (750 ml) of milk to the boil. Mix 1 cup (250 ml) of cold milk with the cornstarch, eggs, sugar, and geranium water in a bowl.

Pour the mixture into the hot milk, while beating vigorously. Cook until you obtain a custard. Spoon some white cream into the goblets of pine nut cream. Leave to cool. Decorate with filberts, pistachios, and almonds if using.

Preparation time:	*20 minutes*		3 cups/350 g	ground almonds
Cooking time:	*10 minutes*		½ tsp	green colorant
Difficulty:	☆		½ tsp	pink colorant

Serves 4

⅔ cup/150 g	superfine sugar
1 sachet	vanilla sugar (or bury a vanilla bean in a container of sugar for a few weeks)
4 tsp/20 ml	rosewater

Bey's *baklawa* is a typical Tunisian sweetmeat. Although the name harks back to the Ottoman presence in this country, it bears absolutely no resemblance to the traditional Turkish *baklava*.

Going back to the 19th century when the beys ruled over Tunisia, this tri-colored confection has been brought up to date over the course of the years. Originally made from marzipan, pistachios, and filberts, bey's *baklawa* are typically diamond shaped.

Easy to make, this specialty is usually made nowadays using just almonds. Originating from Asia, and known by the Romans as "Greek nuts," these oval nuts have a thick, green shell, velvety to the touch, containing one or two seeds. The seeds are eaten fresh or broiled. Marzipan is made from ground almonds and sugar, and is a popular ingredient of cakes and candies.

With the passage of time, pistachios and filberts have been dropped from the recipe, but to maintain the principle of the three colors, Tunisians use vegetable-based food colorants. The use of additives to change the color of a product or dish goes back to ancient times. Even then, people used saffron in their dishes.

To give the syrup its particular flavor, our chef has added rosewater to the mixture. Extracted from a variety of miniature roses, originating from Damascus, the petals are distilled and bring their delicate perfume to many oriental dishes.

Generally served with a selection of other sweetmeats, these delicious candies are mainly served at marriage celebrations. However, it's not uncommon to find them in patisseries. If you want to enjoy bey's *baklawa*, as the Tunisians do, prepare a mint and pine nut tea to go with it.

Prepare the syrup by cooking the superfine sugar, vanilla sugar, and rosewater in 7 tbsp (100 ml) water for 10 minutes.

Sieve the ground almonds. Transfer to a container and pour in the syrup. Mix well with a spatula, and then knead the mixture by hand until you obtain a paste-like consistency.

Split the marzipan into 3 equal portions. Add the green colorant to one portion and knead with your hands to get the colour through. Add the pink colorant to the other portion and knead in the same way. Leave the third portion of the marzipan natural.

Baklawa

Mold the 3 marzipan portions into tubes. Flatten them separately with a rolling pin. Cut them into large, very regular squares.

Place the three marzipan squares on top of each other in this order: lay the pink marzipan square at the bottom, the white on top of the pink, and finally the green on top of the white.

Cut up the baklawa into 1¼ in (3 cm)-wide strips. Cut into very regular diamond shapes. Arrange the bey's baklawa on a dish.

Bouza

Preparation time: *10 minutes*
Cooking time: *10 minutes*
Difficulty: ★

Serves 4

1¼ cups/150 g   blanched pistachios
1 can   condensed milk
3 tbsp   cornstarch

For the decoration:
     pine nuts
     ground almonds
     filberts (hazelnuts)

This delicious pistachio beverage is typically Tunisian. It's often served at *iftar*, the breaking of the Fast of Ramadan at sunset. Easy to digest, it's a very nutritious drink, which fortifies the people during these meager days. Tunisians also drink *bouza* on other occasions, and traditionally it's served while marriage arrangements are being finalized, when the men from the two families meet each other. After they've agreed on the practical details, the hostess offers the famous beverage to celebrate the match. It is a dish that honors the person who drinks it; it shows great respect.

The pistachio is considered to be one of the most refined dried nuts, and is also found in many oriental pastries, in *baklawas*, or in tasty, honey-coated cigar-shaped delicacies. This nut is the seed of the pistachio tree. It originates from Syria, but is also grown in Iraq, Iran, and of course in Tunisia.

Condensed milk is regularly consumed in hot countries. This milk is easy to store and presents no health risk. Moreover, in the past, in countries where the refrigeration procedure was not very well established, such as in Africa, and where fresh milk could not be adequately kept in stock, or simply because there were insufficient dairy cows, this type of milk naturally became the ideal compromise if people wanted a dairy product.

The dried nuts that decorate the top of this delightful drink are as delicate in flavor as the pistachio. Almonds and pine nuts, as well as pistachios, are to be found in many of the pastries in confectioners' shops. Sometimes, filberts take the lion's share, because they are often used to replace the pistachio in making this cream. This filbert cream, which is just as delicious, is called *bellouza*. Tunisians serve it on the same occasions as the *bouza* with pistachios.

Cook the blanched pistachios under your oven broiler for 3–5 minutes. They must stay green. Process them until the nuts form a paste.

Add the condensed milk and add three times its volume in water.

Stir the cornstarch into the mixture. Mix again, stirring vigorously.

with Pistachios

Put the mixture on the heat and cook the bouza, stirring constantly until the beverage thickens.

Pour the bouza into four pretty glasses, sharing equally between each glass.

Decorate the bouza with ground pistachios, pine nuts, and ground almonds. Serve the beverage hot.

Chebbak

Preparation time: 10 minutes
Cooking time: 10 minutes
Difficulty: ★

Serves 4

7/8 cup/100 g	all-purpose flour
3	large eggs
1	lemon
7/8 cup/200 g	sugar

1 tbsp/15 ml	attar of rose oil
	cooking oil

For the decoration:

sesame seeds

The women of Monastir enjoy making *chebbak el Janna*. It's a wonderful excuse to get together in the afternoon, out of the sun, to discuss life in general. In Tunisia, as in most North African countries, gossiping, drinking tea, and eating sweetmeats go hand in hand. These famous cookies are enjoyed throughout the year and you often find hawkers peddling them in the city streets.

They're easy to make and are often prepared at the last minute. For instant success, Mohamed Bouagga advises that you do not immerse the whole mold in the raw dough. Then, when they're dipped in the hot oil, it is much easier to remove the cookies. This way, they'll cook evenly. Otherwise, you'll have to cut out the dough from between the joints with a knife, to remove it from the mold.

The delicate fragrance of these cookies comes from the famous *attarchia*, the oil distilled from the geranium attar of rose. This plant was first introduced to Europe and North Africa from South Africa. In Tunisia it is grown around Nabeul. Its flowers are a very elegant violet color and release a heady fragrance. A large number of sweet Tunisian dishes are flavored with *attarchia*, notably the *masfouf*, which is a sweet couscous.

The translation of *chebbak el Janna* is the very poetic "windows of paradise," probably because the moment you taste them you get a glimpse of paradise! Generally, the designs are geometrical, and must be pleasing to the eye.

Depending on your mood, the broiled sesame seeds sprinkled over the cookies can be substituted with chopped almonds, chocolate shavings, or chocolate flakes. And occasionally, they're even more sumptuous when decorated with gold! Try drizzling a little honey over the "windows of paradise." Serve them at tea time, they're divine!

Sieve the all-purpose flour into a bowl. Break the eggs into the bowl and mix well. Squeeze the juice of 1/2 lemon and place to one side.

Make a syrup with 7/8 cup (200 g) of sugar and 7 tbsp (100 ml) water, ensuring the sugar has dissolved. Add the lemon juice. Cook until "large globules" are formed. Place this syrup to one side.

Add the rose oil to the hot syrup.

el Janna

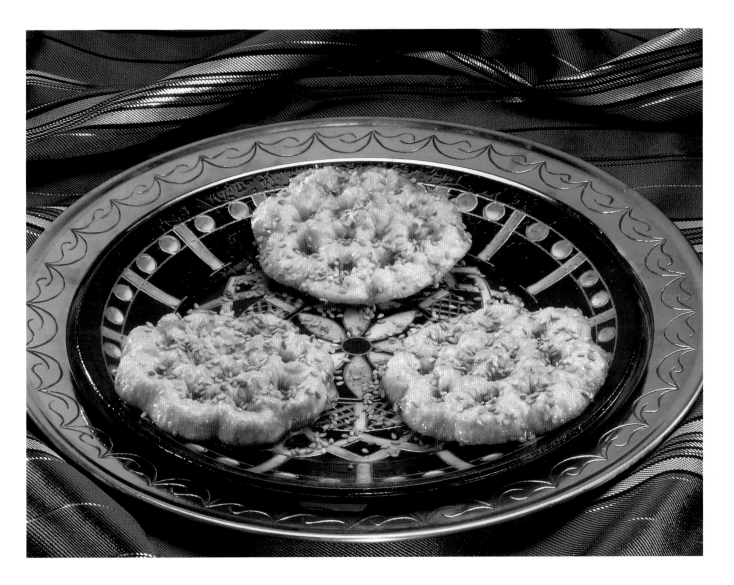

Heat the oil. When it is very hot, dip the molds in the oil. Then dip the molds into the dough without immersing them completely. Immediately transfer the molds to the cooking oil. When partially cooked, the cookies should easily fall away from the molds. Remove when golden brown.

Once cooked, transfer the golden cookies to the hot syrup and soak. Then remove and leave to cool at room temperature.

Sprinkle sesame seeds over the golden brown chebbak el Janna. Allow a minimum of three cookies per person.

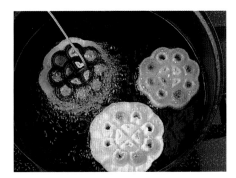

Debla

Preparation time:	40 minutes		1¼ cups/250 g	superfine sugar
Cooking time:	20 minutes		2 tsp/10 ml	orange-flower
Leave dough to stand:	30 minutes			water
Difficulty:	★★		1 tsp	cornstarch

For the decoration:

sesame seeds
ground pistachios

Serves 4

1	egg
⅞ cup/100 g	all-purpose flour
2 tsp	cornstarch
	cooking oil

For the liquid honey syrup:

½	lemon
3½ tbsp/50 g	liquid honey

It's a well-known fact that the best recipes are often invented when a cook has to produce an improvised meal with whatever ingredients are in the cupboard. They have to be bold and innovative.

On that day, did Madame Boccara guess that the recipe she was preparing would be passed into Tunisian culinary heritage? At the time, the question simply didn't arise. This Italian Jewish grandmother, living in Leghorn, Tuscany, was more concerned about making a sweetmeat for some unexpected guests. All she had in the cupboard were a few eggs and some flour. With these basic ingredients, she made a dough, rolling it into an original shape. Then she plunged these "donuts" into boiling oil. Thinking that these "donuts" were a little dry and tasteless, in a moment of inspiration she coated them with liquid honey. It was the beginning of the 19th century and the *manicotti* had just been created.

Many years later, Madame Boccara's four daughters went to live in Tunisia, like many Italian Jews. They continued to make this pastry, carrying on their mother's creation. The family recipe became more sophisticated and flavors were added—notably orange-flower water was mixed with the liquid honey. They also decorated the *manicotti* with sesame seeds or ground pistachios.

Adopted by the whole of the Jewish community in Tunis, these excellent pastries then passed into Tunisian culinary heritage. Called *debla* in Arabic, they are also known as *wednin el kadhi*, which means "judge's ear."

A great favorite of the Tunisians, *debla* are usually served at family gatherings. Madame Boccara would certainly have been proud to learn that her improvised sweetmeat would be remembered two centuries later.

Prepare the debla *dough by mixing an egg into the all-purpose flour in a bowl. Mix well.*

Knead the mixture with your hands until you obtain a consistent dough. If the dough sticks, add a little more all-purpose flour. Leave the dough to stand wrapped in a dry piece of linen for 30 minutes.

Sprinkle 1 tsp cornstarch over the work area. Knead the dough. Reshape it into a ball, and continue to knead while sprinkling with cornstarch. Spread it out with a rolling pin, turning it over several times. Put it through the dough machine to make a thin layer.

Cut up the dough into long ribbons. Prepare the syrup by squeezing the ½ lemon. Cook it with the liquid honey, superfine sugar, orange-flower water, cornstarch, and 1¼ cups (300 ml) water. Cook until the sugar dissolves.

Wedge a ribbon of dough between your forefinger and middle finger, then wind it up between your fingers. Repeat with the remaining dough ribbons.

Gently immerse a debla in the hot cooking oil. When cooked, drain the excess oil on a paper towel. Soak each cooked debla in the liquid honey syrup. Create variety by decorating some with sesame seeds and some with ground pistachios, and leave others plain.

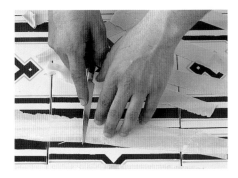

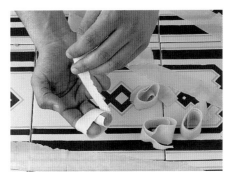

Ghrïba with

Preparation time: 35 minutes
Cooking time: 20 minutes
To cool the dough: 30 minutes
Difficulty: ☆

Serves 4

³/₄ cup/150 g unsalted butter
¹/₃ cup/80 g all-purpose flour
1³/₄ cups/250 g garbanzo bean (chickpea) flour

⁷/₈ cup/100 g confectioners' sugar
1 tbsp/15 ml vegetable oil

The *ghrïba homs* is a popular pastry. This specialty, made with garbanzo bean flour, is a great favorite of the people in the Tunis region, and is mainly enjoyed at the *Aïd el fitr*, celebrating the breaking of the Fast of Ramadan.

Cooking these small cakes is a very delicate operation. In many Tunisian households, the women make the dough, but then the dough is put on a large plate and taken to the neighborhood baker by the men. According to Mohamed Korbi, this is a wonderful spectacle in the streets of Tunis: "There are endless lines outside the bakeries. Everyone spends the time talking to each other and exchanging news. The perfume from the *ghrïba homs* fills the air, already heralding the feast which is being prepared."

The outstanding stars of these delights are garbanzo beans, called *homs* in Arabic. Originally from west Asia, and mentioned by Homer in *The Iliad*, these leguminous plants are to be found in many oriental dishes. The dry, hot climate of the Mediterranean region provides just the right conditions for their cultivation. Ground into flour, the round, dented, beige-colored grains have an aftertaste of filberts. According to our chef, you can also make the *ghrïba* dough with sorghum, a cereal much enjoyed by the Tunisians.

Although you need to be really careful when cooking the dough, it's also essential to keep an eye on the preparation of the nut-colored butter. Under no circumstances should the butter be allowed to burn.

Our chef suggests giving the dish a touch of originality by making an orange sauce to accompany it, thereby evoking sunny Tunisian landscapes.

Melt the unsalted butter over a low heat in a saucepan. Remove the whey. Brown the unsalted butter until it becomes nut-colored, but take care not to burn it.

Sieve the white all-purpose flour, the garbanzo bean flour, and the confectioners' sugar separately.

Mix the two flours, the confectioners' sugar and the nut-colored butter in a dish. Mix well by hand, gradually incorporating all the dry ingredients.

Garbanzo Beans

Continue to knead the mixture with your hands until you have a consistent yet crumbly dough. Use the heat of your palms to warm this dough.

Lay the dough on the work area and roll it into tubes. Lengthen the shapes into rolls of approximately ³/₄ in (15 mm) in diameter.

Cut diagonally with a knife, pieces measuring 2¹/₄ in (5.5 cm) long. Carefully arrange the ghrïba on a greased plate. Chill in the refrigerator for 30 minutes. Cook in the oven at 265 °F/130 °C for 15–20 minutes. Allow to cool before arranging them on your dish.

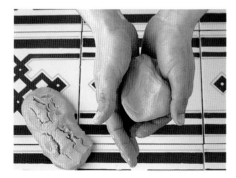

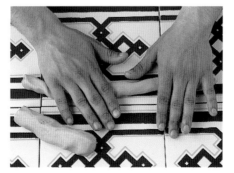

H'rissa

Preparation time: 1 hour
Cooking time: 15 minutes
Leave the semolina paste
    to stand: 20 minutes
Difficulty: ★

Serves 4

5 cups/1 kg	large-grained semolina
³/₄ cup/200 g	unsalted butter
2 cups/500 ml	milk
3 cups/500 g	dates
2 cups/250 g	*chamia*
1¹/₄ cups/250 g	sugar
4¹/₂ cups/500 g	white ground almonds

For the decoration:

1¹/₂ cups/200 g	walnuts
1¹/₂ cups/200 g	pistachios
1¹/₂ cups/200 g	almonds

Originally from the northwestern and southern regions of Tunisia, *h'rissa hloua* is a dessert made of browned semolina, almonds, dates, pistachios, and *chamia*. Children enjoy eating this sweetmeat after breakfast.

The only difficulty with this recipe is the preparation of the semolina—it must not be allowed to burn under any circumstances. Some families will use liquid honey instead of sugar, stirring it in at the end of cooking. Our chef suggests that you could flavor the semolina with orange-flower water when you're kneading it. A word of warning—*h'rissa hloua* will keep for only two days.

The presence of *chamia* in this pastry from the northwest of Tunisia remains a mystery to our chef. *Chamia*, a candy made from oil and ground sesame seeds, takes its name from Cham, in Syria, where it is produced. About 50 years ago, *chamia* was only available in the large cities, such as Tunis.

The northern villagers probably bought their *chamia* when they were away from home. On their return, they would present their wives with this sweet delicacy. In return, their wives added it to other sugary delights and served their husbands *h'rissa hloua*. If *chamia* is unavailable, its very oriental sweetness can be created by using liquid honey instead.

Dates, on the other hand, are essential in this dessert. With its palm groves and oases, this fruit is inextricably linked with Tunisia's culinary heritage. Select the *deglet el nour* variety in preference, which are often presented under the label "dates from Tunis." Their light, translucent color and unique flavor have earned them the nickname, the date of sunshine and light.

The *h'rissa hloua* is an ideal sweetmeat for families to enjoy, accompanied by the traditional glass of mint tea.

Brown the semolina gently in a copper saucepan by stirring it with a spatula for approximately 10 minutes.

Melt ⁵/₈ cup/180 g of the unsalted butter in a saucepan. Boil the milk. Add the melted butter to the semolina in the saucepan, and then add the hot milk. Stir well.

Pit the dates and cut into strips. Remove the saucepan from the heat, and add the dates to the semolina. Add the chamia, sugar and ground almonds. Leave to stand for 20 minutes.

Hloua

Knead the mixture with your hands to form a paste.

Grease the plate with the rest of the unsalted butter and spread out the paste with a metal spatula.

Decorate with the walnuts, pistachios, and the almonds cut into 2 lengthwise. Cut into diamond shapes. Arrange the diamond shapes on the plate.

Jaouia

Preparation time: 50 minutes
Cooking time: 50 minutes
Difficulty: ✶

Serves 4

1/2 cup/50 g	filberts (hazelnuts)
1 1/4 cups/150 g	blanched almonds
1/2 cup/50 g	walnuts
1/4 cup/20 g	pistachios
1/4 cup/25 g	pine nuts
1 tbsp/15 ml	vegetable oil

For the syrup:

3/4 cup/150 g	superfine sugar
1 sachet	vanilla sugar (bury a vanilla bean in a container of sugar for a few weeks)
1/2	lemon (juice of)

For the decoration:

ground pistachios
pine nuts

In Tunisia, the *jaouia* enjoys a special status. Considered to be a luxury dish, according to legend this pastry made from dried nuts was the bey's favorite sweetmeat. A symbol of wealth, today it is mainly served at marriage celebrations.

Dried nuts were already a great favorite of the Egyptians, Greeks, and Romans. Thanks to the nutritional value and high-calorie content concentrated in a very small nut, dried nuts are saturated with sunshine. Deliciously and naturally sweetened, they're rich in carbohydrates, vitamins, mineral salts, lipids, and even proteins.

Although walnuts are generally used to decorate oriental pastries, they are included in the ingredients for *jaouia*. These nuts, encased in a hard shell, contain a kernel with two halves, covered with a thin, relatively dark yellow film. To restore their youthful appearance, you can soak dried

nuts for a few hours in a container of hot milk. The film will come off by itself, restoring the attractive appearance of the flesh. For this recipe, the nuts must be ground. Don't be tempted to grind them in the blender, as the speed of the blade has the effect of removing the flavor of the oil.

Filberts, another ingredient in this pastry, are distinguished by their delicate flavor. These nuts from the hazel tree have a hard shell, containing an egg-shaped or round seed. Once they're shelled, filberts must be kept in a dark, dry place so that they don't go rancid. Both whole and ground filberts are used.

When the sugar has been cooked and mixed with the dried nuts, the *jaouia* resembles a nougatine. This Tunisian pastry, which is very high in calories, will appeal to children, giving them the energy they require.

Prepare the dried nuts separately by cooking them in the oven at 275 °F/ 140 °C: the filberts for approximately 20 minutes; the almonds for 15 minutes; then the walnuts for 5 minutes. Remove the skin of the broiled filberts.

With a rolling pin, roughly grind the almonds, walnuts, filberts, pistachios, and pine nuts.

For the syrup, heat the sugars with 7 tbsp (100 ml) water. Bring to the boil, and add the lemon juice. To check whether the syrup's cooked, dip the blade of a knife in cold water, then in the syrup, then back in the cold water. The syrup should form a soft ball between your fingers.

Pour the syrup over the dried, ground nuts and stir well with a wooden spatula.

Lightly grease the work area and rolling pin with vegetable oil. Lay the jaouia out and flatten it. Repeat the procedure on a tray.

Cut out generous strips of jaouia on the tray and then cut them into squares. Decorate by gently dipping the surface of the jaouia squares into the ground pistachios. Top with a pine nut. Arrange the jaouia on a dish.

Kâber

Preparation time:	20 minutes
Cooking time:	10 minutes
Difficulty:	✫

Serves 4

2½ cups/300 g	ground almonds
¾ cup/150 g	superfine sugar
1 sachet	vanilla sugar (bury a vanilla bean in a container of sugar for a few weeks)
4 tsp/20 ml	rosewater
½ tsp	green colorant
½ tsp	pink colorant

For the decoration:

superfine sugar
pine nuts (optional)

Kâber ellouz means "almond ball" in Arabic. Very easy to make, the history of this sweetmeat is worthy of being included in the *Tales from 1,001 Arabian Nights*.

Legend has it that a very long time ago, an evil spirit deprived Tunisia of its dates. The sultan who reigned at that time was a cruel man. Only date pastries had the power to soften his nature. As the days passed, date reserves continued to diminish. One of the desperate palace cooks thought she could deceive the sultan's taste buds, so she prepared some small balls made of marzipan, pistachios, and filberts. Discovering her trickery, the king beheaded her. Appalled at the thought of suffering the same fate, another cook threw the remaining balls into a sack of sugar. The *kâber ellouz* were born…

In Tunisia, these delightful treats are mainly served on important feast days, at engagements, marriages, or circumcisions. As is the case with many of these recipes, marzipan is the star ingredient. Essentially grown in the Sfax region, the almond tree blossoms in the spring, and is recognizable by its magnificent white flowers. The first, sweet, fresh almonds have a subtle flavor. On the other hand, dried almonds, which you find whole, split, ground, in the form of a paste, or even a cream, are an ingredient of many cakes, cookies, candies, and confectionery.

Well, according to the legend, the sugar saved the second cook's head. This sweet-flavored substance forms naturally in the leaves of many plants and is concentrated in their roots or stems. In North Africa, sugar is extracted from the date palm. But the most commonly used is cane sugar. Thousands of years ago, Asians were already using sugar in the form of cane syrup, while Europeans were eating honey.

Prepare the paste by sieving the ground almonds.

Make the syrup by cooking the superfine sugar, and the vanilla sugar in 7 tbsp (100 ml) water for 10 minutes. Stir in the rosewater. Pour the syrup into the ground almonds and blend with a spatula.

Using your fingers, knead the paste on the work area.

Ellouz

Split the marzipan into 3 equal portions. Add the green colorant to one part and knead to mix the color through. Color the second part with the pink colorant in the same way. Leave the third part natural.

Roll each colored batch onto a work area to thin it out. Make 3 sausage-shapes measuring ³/₄ in (2 cm) in diameter. Create a tri-colored braid from the parts.

Cut the braid into approximately 1 oz/ 20 g pieces. Roll them between the palms of your hands to form consistent, smooth balls. Coat the kâber ellouz with superfine sugar to finish. Serve in a pile on a plate, decorated with pine nuts, if using.

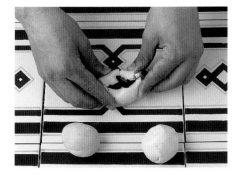

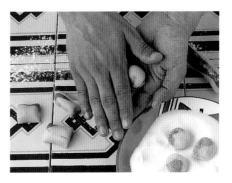

Preparation time:	*30 minutes*
Cooking time:	*30 minutes*
Difficulty:	★★

Serves 4

1¼ cups/150 g	almonds
1¼ cups/150 g	filberts (hazelnuts)
½ cup/50 g	pine nuts
2½ cups/500 g	sugar
1	lemon

1 trickle	geranium water
½ cup/100 g	unsalted butter
12	*malsouka* sheets
½ cup/50 g	ground pistachios

Our chef's mother, Leïla, inspired Ali to create this recipe, which is crunchy and yet melts in the mouth, and is highly flavored. The *ourta* is one of the great family of Tunisian pastries, a tasty combination of Turkish, Greek, and Andalucian influences.

Most of these delights are hidden in a *malsouka* sheet. Prepared with semolina and thickened with a very small amount of egg and water, the batter is stirred until smooth, and then a large copper dish is heated on a charcoal stove. The slightly runny batter is very slowly poured onto the very hot plate, until a large, extremely thin sheet of batter is obtained. The batter must be cooked until it is crispy and crumbly.

Factory-made *malsouka* sheets are a very practical solution if you want to make the *ourta* quickly. But the chef prefers to make his own. Actually, he feels that the commercially produced batter, made from flour and eggs, is not fine enough and is a little hard. He also takes the precaution of laying two sheets at the bottom of the mold to stiffen the cake, and it also enables him to remove one of the layers, should the bottom layer burn.

Ali Matri grinds the almonds and filberts only roughly, to keep a slightly crunchy texture. When preparing the *ourta*, he sprinkles just a few pine nuts over the almonds and filberts, and keeps the rest for decoration.

In the northeast of Tunisia, the Cap Bon peninsula abounds in bitter orange trees and geraniums, which are destined for the production of flower water. Actually, this country produces numerous extracts—rose, thyme, orange-flower, and geranium among others. Our *ourta* is enhanced with wild geranium-flower water, which gives this dessert a completely unexpected flavor.

Broil the almonds, filberts, and pine nuts separately on a tray under the oven broiler. Grind the almonds and filberts roughly in the food processor bowl. Place whole pine nuts to one side.

Pour the sugar and a glass of water into a heavy-duty saucepan. Squeeze a piece of lemon into it. Cook over quite a high heat, until the sugar dissolves and you obtain a syrup. Take the pan off the heat and mix in the geranium water. Stir well.

Using a brush, coat the inside of a round cake mold with melted butter. Place a malsouka *sheet on the base. Brush this with the melted butter. Place another sheet on top, and coat this with butter, too.*

Ourta

Sprinkle some of the chopped dried nuts over the malsouka sheets. Sprinkle with a few pine nuts. Place another malsouka sheet on top, brush with melted butter, sprinkle with dried nuts … until you've used up all the ingredients. Finish with a malsouka sheet coated in butter.

Bake the cake for approximately 10 minutes in the oven, until the surface is golden brown and crispy. As soon as it's cooked, take it out of the oven and drizzle it with geranium syrup.

When the cake has thoroughly absorbed all the syrup, turn it out carefully onto a serving plate. Sprinkle it with ground pistachios and the rest of the broiled pine nuts.

Chamia Parfait

Preparation time: 30 minutes
Cooking time: 10 minutes
To chill: 24 hours
Difficulty: ★★

Serves 4

1⅛ cup/250 ml	light whipping cream
4	eggs
¼ cup/50 g	sugar
5 tbsp/70 g	*chamia* (or *halva*)
1	lemon
6 tsp/30 g	sesame seeds

For the orange sauce:

7	Tunisian blood oranges
1 tsp	cornstarch
3 tbsp/45 g	superfine sugar

For the garnish:

	mint for decoration

Chamia parfait is a recent Tunisian creation and can be distinguished from classic French parfaits. It is the sesame paste called *chamia*, or *halva*, that gives the dish its typically eastern flavor. As ice cream doesn't feature very much in the traditional culinary customs of Tunisia, this creation of our chef is very welcome.

Readily available in the whole of the Mediterranean region, *chamia* is a factory-made mixture produced from sesame seeds, sugar, and various other products. Sometimes, dried nuts such as almonds, pistachios, and filberts are added to the mixture. To break it up before adding it to the ice cream, place in a sieve above a bowl, and crush it through with the back of a spoon.

As when making sponge cake, the blended eggs and sugar must be beaten in a basin placed over a saucepan of hot water to produce a thick cream; then continue to beat it off

the heat, until the mixture cools down. The well-chilled whipped cream is added to the mixture after the *chamia*, so that it doesn't lose its thick consistency.

When the mixture has been freezing for 3 hours, remember to stir the parfait with a fork. If you prefer, instead of pouring the parfait into individual molds, you can place it in a cake mold, lined with plastic wrap. When it's very cold, turn out the parfait and cut it into slices.

The citrus fruit sauce is prepared with one of the best oranges in the world: the Tunisian blood orange is a semi-blood orange harvested from January to April in the Cap Bon peninsula, from Tunis to Bizerte, and in the Kairouan region. Juicy and fragrant, it has an oval or round shape, and its delicately colored, smooth skin is easy to peel when it ripens. Generally, there are no pits in these oranges. Thompson oranges are a suitable alternative.

First make the parfait. Beat the well-chilled light whipping cream until thick.

Break 2 whole eggs and 2 yolks in a basin. Stir in the sugar. Place over a saucepan of simmering hot water, and beat until the mixture turns pale and thickens.

Take off the heat, and crumble the chamia into the egg cream. Add a few lemon shavings. Blend gently so that the mixture doesn't lose volume. Cool.

and Orange Sauce

When the chamia cream is very cold, incorporate the whipped cream, gently folding it in to form the parfait mixture.

Place a piece of plastic wrap in individual small molds. With a tablespoon, fill each mold with parfait. Freeze for 24 hours. For the sauce, squeeze 5 of the oranges and mix the juice and the cornstarch in a saucepan.

Stir in the sugar, and mix. Bring gently to the boil until the sauce thickens. Allow to cool down. Turn out the parfaits onto plates. Decorate with peeled orange quarters, sesame seeds, and mint. Surround the parfait with the orange sauce.

Palm Grove

Preparation time: 40 minutes
Difficulty: ★

Serves 4

2¹/₂ cups/400 g	*alig* dates
3 slices	sandwich bread
3¹/₂ tbsp/50 ml	olive oil

¹/₄ cup/50 g	salted butter
¹/₂ cup/100 g	superfine sugar

Renowned for its magnificent palm grove, the oasis of Tozeur extends over more than 2,470 acres (1,000 hectares). In this southwest region of Tunisia, many people still earn their living from the date harvest. This providential fruit is therefore found in many recipes.

Palm grove *rfiss* is a great favorite of nomads. When they're on the move, shepherds, camel drivers, and goatherds carry this candy in their *mokhla*, a small, woven, woollen bag, and they enjoy it with a glass of milk.

Easy to make, palm grove *rfiss* is essentially made of chopped dates, sugar, salted butter, olive oil, and breadcrumbs. It's very high in calories, and this dessert has the advantage of keeping for several days.

Tozeur oasis is renowned for the quality of its dates. Only the female palm trees bear the fruit. Our chef has chosen the *alig* variety for this recipe. They're mahogany in color, and quite large with a smooth, semi-dry skin, and an exceptionally sweet flavor. If you don't use fresh dates, the chef advises you to blanch the dates for 1–2 minutes in boiling water.

To make a success of this recipe, the salted butter must be at room temperature. In Tunisian cuisine, salted butter is mainly served as a condiment and brings its slightly sharp flavor to dishes and pastries.

For the breadcrumbs, you can use roasted, fine semolina instead of sandwich bread.

In the past, when feminine curves were a measure of beauty, the women of Tozeur ate the palm grove *rfiss* without restraint. Nowadays, this very oriental delight is still enjoyed, but with a lot more moderation!

Pit the dates and chop them finely in a grinder.

Break the slices of bread into small pieces and make breadcrumbs. Add to the chopped dates and mix with your fingers.

Add the olive oil and mix well with your fingers.

Rfiss

Add the salted butter and mix to form a paste.

Add ¼ cup (50 g) of the superfine sugar. Mix again.

Make the small balls into equal sizes and roll them between the palms of your hands. Sprinkle the rest of the sugar over the rfiss and roll them between your palms. Arrange the rfiss in a large dish.

Rfissa with

Preparation time:	*15 minutes*
Cooking time:	*25 minutes*
Difficulty:	★

Serves 4

1¼ cups/200 g	fine semolina
¾ cup/200 ml	olive oil
1½ cups/250 g	dates
½ cup/50 g	confectioners' sugar
	salt

For the decoration of your choice:

½ cup/50 g	shelled pistachios
½ cup/50 g	almonds
½ cup/50 g	filberts (hazelnuts)
½ cup/50 g	pine nuts
4	prickly pears

A traditional specialty from Kairouan, the *rfissa* is one of the customary sweetmeats served in the evening during the month of Ramadan. It's accompanied by fermented milk or *lben*. For the rest of the year, it's enjoyed at breakfast with coffee.

Durum wheat semolina, the base of this recipe, must always be of extremely good quality. Tunisians also make another very similar pastry, the *makroud*: this is made with semolina and dates, and molded into small cakes and fried.

The dates, which grace the *rfissa*, are one of the main crop exports from Tunisia. Dates are the third most important Tunisian agricultural specialty marketed throughout the world, after olive oil and fish products. Palm trees are mainly planted out in the south of the country, around Chott el Jerid, and provide more than 105,000 tons (95,000 tonnes) of dates a year. The oases of Tozeur, Kebili, and Tamerza are particularly renowned for the quality and abundance of their fruits.

Approximately 150 varieties ripen under the Tunisian sun, but only four varieties are exported: the *deglet nour* (75% of plantations); the *kenta*; the *khuwat*, and the *alig*. Chokri Chteoui prefers very fresh *alig* dates for this recipe. Smooth and very sweet, *alig* dates are long and mahogany in color. Their soft flesh makes them easy to crush when they're mixed with the semolina. As they ripen in November, he uses dried dates for the rest of the year, which must be rehydrated before use.

The olive oil should be of impeccable quality. People living in the countryside generally use a very dense "house" oil, which is pressed in a stone mill. Instead of dates you can use soaked dried figs, and decorate the *rfissa* with ground pistachios, almonds, filberts, or pine nuts.

Pour the semolina into a dish. Lightly salt it. Sprinkle it with 7 tbsp (100 ml) of the olive oil and a little water. Knead it until a thick paste forms.

Grease a baking sheet. Spread the semolina over the sheet with the flat of your hand. As soon as the paste is firm, shape the edges so that you have a rough rectangle. Brown in the oven at 430 °F/ 220 °C for 25 minutes.

Meanwhile cut the dates into 2 halves. Remove the pits. Cut up into fine strips with a small knife.

Dates from Kairouan

When cooked, cut the semolina paste into medium-sized pieces. Grind it in a mortar, using a pestle.

Add the pieces of dates to the ground semolina paste. Blend, using your fingertips. Take a little of the mixture in your hand, knead, and let the semolina trickle slowly into the dish. Repeat several times.

Pour the confectioners' sugar and then trickle the remaining olive oil into the mixture. Blend the whole mixture thoroughly. Fill the bowl of a large ladle with the mixture, pack down, and turn out onto a plate. Sprinkle with crushed pistachios, or any of the nuts you choose.

Fig Samsa with

Preparation time: 35 minutes
Cooking time: 20–25 minutes
To soak the figs: 30 minutes
Difficulty: ★★

Serves 4

1¼ cups/200 g	dried figs
5	oranges
3 tbsp/40 ml	liquid honey
½ tsp	superfine sugar (optional)
2	eggs, separated
1 cup/100 g	ground almonds
2 tbsp/30 ml	orange-flower water

5	feuilles de brick (or use filo pastry)

1½ tbsp/20 g	unsalted butter, melted
⅜ cup/50 g	confectioners' sugar
a little	peanut oil, for greasing

For the sauce:

juice of 3	blood oranges
1	pinch cornstarch

For the decoration:

4	fresh figs (optional)

The Cap Bon peninsula is the most immense orchard in Tunisia. Nabeul, the native town of our chef, is also renowned for its camel markets, craft center, fig trees, orange groves, and much more…

By reviving this recipe, Rafik Tlatli wanted to share the diversity of regional products, which are so invaluable to the culinary heritage of Nabeul. *Samsa* are usually made with ground almonds and egg white.

Every year, the business community of Nabeul organizes the orange festival. Among the varieties grown in this region are the blood oranges, also known as "Maltese oranges." Spherical in shape, they reveal a bright red, juicy pulp. Select bright, heavy oranges. These sought-after citrus fruits are quite hardy and keep for several days at room temperature. Our chef wanted to accompany the *samsa* with a blood orange sauce because of the unique, slightly sour flavor of the oranges. However, according to the season, you can make it with berry sauce instead.

Figs are believed to have originally come from the Orient, and are much enjoyed by the Mediterranean people, who eat them fresh or dried. Figs are very nourishing and rich in sugar and vitamins. To dry them, they are left in the sun, then washed in sea water, and then sterilized. The best dried figs are entwined with a piece of raffia. They can be eaten plain, or stuffed with almonds or walnuts. You can also make the *samsa* stuffing with the pulp of fresh figs, which is light and excellent.

Tunisian culinary expertise is rediscovered in the creation of the *samsa*. These small, delicate, pastry parcels, accompanied by a blood orange sauce, reveal a subtle union of sweet and slightly acidic flavors—an oriental delicacy that is a delight for gourmets!

Soak the figs in cold water for 30 minutes. Squeeze the 5 oranges to produce 1¼ cups (300 ml) juice. Blend the figs with the orange juice, honey, and sugar. Pour this mixture into a saucepan and slowly bring to the boil for approximately 10 minutes.

Allow to cool and fold in most of the egg white, ground almonds, and orange-flower water. Place a little egg white to one side for making the parcels.

With the point of a large knife, cut the feuille de brick into strips of approximately 2½ in (6 cm) in width.

Blood Orange Sauce

Arrange the strips over a work area and share out the fig mixture, placing it at the beginning of each strip.

Fold the strip into a triangle, by rolling once to the left and once to the right to seal the sides. Stick the end of each triangle down with a little of the reserved egg white. Grease the dish and coat the samsa with melted butter.

Bake in the oven at 350 °F/180 °C for approximately 10 minutes. Dust with confectioners' sugar. Make the sauce: Heat the blood orange juice and stir in the cornstarch until thick. Place the samsa on a plate with the sauce. Decorate with fresh figs.

Takoua with

Preparation time:	25 minutes
Cooking time:	5 minutes
Difficulty:	✳

Serves 4

2¹/₂ cups/500 g	sesame seeds
3	oranges
7 tbsp/100 ml	orange-flower water
¹/₂ cup/100 g	superfine sugar
⁷/₈ cup/100 g	confectioners' sugar

For the decoration:

mint leaves

The *takoua* with orange-flower water is a traditional dessert from the Bizerte region. This easy-to-make specialty was originally prepared in Jewish families to celebrate Shabbat (the Jewish Sabbath).

These small balls made from sesame seeds are a real delight. For this preparation, the sesame seeds must be sorted by hand to remove impurities. The sesame is an oleaginous plant and its minuscule oval seeds are often used to garnish oriental pastries, such as the *halva*, along with honey and almonds. In addition, sesame oil is much enjoyed in the Mediterranean region, and particularly in the Middle East.

The orange flavor is optional in this recipe. Orange-flower water is blended with sesame seeds, and brings its mellow flavors to the dish. To make orange-flower water the flowers are gathered from the bitter orange tree, and then distilled. This delicately flavored water is used to flavor many Tunisian dishes. In some families from Bizerte, the *takoua* are made with geranium water or rosewater instead.

For his part, our chef opted to base this recipe on the orange by making juice and decorating the plates with orange segments. In Tunisia, orange groves stretch as far as the eye can see. These winter fruits are renowned for their vitamin A and C content. According to the variety, their flavor is relatively sweet, slightly acidic, or fragrant. Preferably choose bright, heavy fruits. As they're quite hardy, they keep for several days at room temperature.

This dessert is particularly rich. However, you can add a little unsalted butter, so that it melts in the mouth even more. Serve *takoua* with orange-flower water at any time with the traditional glass of mint tea.

Arrange the sesame seeds over the work area and sort them with your hands to remove impurities. Rinse in water and drain. Allow them to dry for approximately 10 minutes.

Brown the sesame seeds in a frying pan, while stirring with a wooden spatula. Squeeze 2 of the oranges and keep the juice to one side for the decoration. Thoroughly peel the remaining orange and remove the segments for the decoration.

Put the sesame seeds into the food processor and pour in the orange-flower water. Blend at a high speed.

Orange-Flower Water

Add the confectioners' sugar to the mixture. Blend until a paste is formed.

Spread out the paste on a dish and let it stand for a few moments.

Pour the confectioners' sugar over the work area and roll up the sesame paste with your hands to make balls. Arrange the mint leaves on the plates and place the takoua on top of them. Pour a little orange juice onto the plates and decorate with the reserved orange segments.

Tarayoune

Preparation time: 40 minutes
Cooking time: 25 minutes
Refrigeration of the mixture: 5 minutes
Difficulty: ★★

Serves 4

⁵/₈ cup/70 g	all-purpose flour
3¹/₂ tbsp/50 g	superfine sugar
2 cups/500 ml	milk
2 tsp/10 ml	jasmine flower water
1 trickle	olive oil
1 cup/100 g	ground pistachios
4	eggs, separated
³/₈ cup/50 g	confectioners' sugar

For the pistachio sauce:

5	eggs, separated
¹/₂ cup/100 g	superfine sugar
2 cups/500 ml	hot milk
¹/₂ cup/50 g	ground pistachios

For the decoration:

	ground pistachios

Tarayoune is a traditional Tunisian dessert. According to legend, it owes its name to an aristocrat not very familiar with military ranks. Originally, this dessert, consisting of a white layer, another green layer made from pistachios, then a covering of zabaglione, was known by the name *kholozek el lioua*, or the colonel's cake. During a society evening, the aristocrat confused the colors of military stripes, and offered his guests this "skirmisher's cake," otherwise known as *tarayoune*. This name stuck.

In Tunisian families, this fairly substantial dessert is served all year round. Pistachios, which color the central part of the *tarayoune*, are found in many oriental and Mediterranean dishes. The pistachio tree, which grows in Tunisia, originates from Syria. The small, greenish seeds are lodged in a shell, which opens when the fruit is ripe. Next, the pistachios are cut out by hand and then soaked to remove their thick husk, and finally dried in the sun. Renowned for their subtle flavor, they give the *tarayoune* their distinctive character.

This delicious specialty is flavored with jasmine water. The wonderfully fragrant plant jasmine abounds in Tunisia, and is a sophisticated symbol of the country. As an alternative, you can use rosewater or geranium water, also commonly found in the Nabeul region.

Usually, the *tarayoune* is prepared on a large plate, and then cut into squares. Our chef suggests presenting it in individual portions, decorated with a check pattern of ground pistachios. You also make the pistachio sauce with ground pistachios, which are central to this recipe; it would be a wonderful accompaniment to this colonel's dessert, which became the dessert of a skirmisher!

Prepare the tarayoune by blending the all-purpose flour, superfine sugar, and the milk in a container. Beat with a whisk.

Pour the mixture through the strainer. Next prepare the pistachio sauce by mixing 5 egg yolks with the superfine sugar. Blend until pale with a whisk. Add the hot milk. Add the ground pistachios and cook for 5 minutes. Sieve. Allow to stand and place to one side.

Cook the tarayoune over a low heat while blending continuously. Add the jasmine flower water. Blend until the mixture thickens a little.

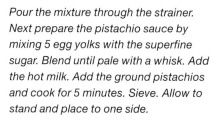

with Pistachio Sauce

Lightly grease a large plate with olive oil. Pour the tarayoune mixture into the cake pans. Allow to cool. Put in the refrigerator for 5 minutes.

Sprinkle a layer of ground pistachios over the cake pans.

Prepare the zabaglione by beating the 4 egg yolks and the confectioners' sugar. Pour the mixture over the tarayoune. Bake in the oven at 210 °F/100 °C for 10 mins. Turn out of the cake pans, and arrange on a plate. Decorate with ground pistachios and pour the pistachio sauce around.

Touagin

Preparation time:	40 minutes
Cooking time:	35 minutes
Difficulty:	★

Serves 4

1	lemon
2½ cups/300 g	ground almonds
⅞ cup/95 g	confectioners' sugar
2	eggs

For the decoration:

pistachios
confectioners' sugar

The *touagin* with almonds are delicious and attractively decorated petits fours. Originally made exclusively for the bey, Tunisians consider them to be one of the most sophisticated pastries. Although they're quite easy to make, the preparation of the *touagin* does require patience. Each individual shape must be modeled before cooking.

Almonds, a major ingredient of this recipe, are directly associated with oriental cuisine. The almond is egg-shaped, green, and velvety to the touch, and its shell contains one or two seeds. Originating from Asia, they're also available dried.

Grown in Tunisia, the lemon flavors savory dishes and pastries perfectly. This citrus fruit, known for its high vitamin C content, will keep between one and two weeks in the refrigerator in the crisper. To make the peel, preferably select unwaxed varieties.

Our chef is particularly insistent on the decoration of the *touagin*. Decoration is essential. Once they've cooled, you must coat the petits fours with confectioners' sugar. This is a crystallized sugar, very useful in pastry-making, that is ground very finely into powder, and then starch is added to avoid it setting into a solid block.

The final touch to these petits fours is again the famous pistachios, which are so dear to the Tunisian heart. Some people believe that the first pistachio trees were planted on Mediterranean shores more than 2,000 years ago. The small greenish colored seeds, which stem from these trees, have a sweet flavor and are packed with potassium, copper, and magnesium.

To accentuate the delicacy of these *touagin* with almonds, we suggest you decorate your table with flowers, to give an oriental atmosphere.

Thoroughly peel the lemon. Chop the peel into very small pieces. Prepare the dough by putting the ground almonds, ¾ cup (90 g) of confectioners' sugar, the eggs and lemon peel into a bowl.

Mix and knead with your hands until you have a smooth and consistent dough.

Mold the dough into tubes. Roll them out and lengthen them until they're 1¾ in (4 cm) in diameter.

with Almonds

Cut the tubes up into small, very regular pieces. Grind the pistachios and place them to one side for the decoration.

Using tart tongs, pinch around the pieces of dough. Gently push your finger into the top of the pieces to make a dent.

Sprinkle the baking sheet with the remaining confectioners' sugar and arrange the touagin. Bake at 265 °F/ 130 °C for 35 minutes. Allow to cool, then roll in the confectioners' sugar. Sprinkle each with a dash of pistachios. Arrange the touagin on a dish.

The Chefs

Mimoun Arroum

Chedly Azzaz

Mohamed Bouagga

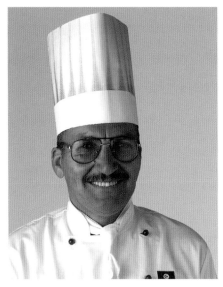

Mohamed Boujelben

Mohamed Boussabeh

Chokri Chteoui

Mohamed Korbi

Sabri Kouki

Moez Ksouda

Ali Matri

Rafik Tlatli

Fethi Tounsi

Abbreviations:

1 oz = 1 ounce = 28 grams
1 lb = 1 pound = 16 ounces
1 cup = 8 ounces *(see below)
1 cup = 8 fluid ounces = 250 ml (liquids)
2 cups = 1 pint (liquids)
1 glass = 4–6 fluid ounces = 125–150 ml (liquids)
1 tbsp = 1 level tablespoon = 15–20 g *(see below) = 15 ml (liquids)
1 tsp = 1 level teaspoon = 3–5 g *(see below) = 5 ml (liquids)

1 kg = 1 kilogram = 1000 grams
1 g = 1 gram = $^{1}/_{1000}$ kilogram
1 l = 1 liter = 1000 milliliters = approx. 34 fluid ounces
1 ml = 1 milliliter = $^{1}/_{1000}$ liter

*The weight of dry ingredients varies significantly depending on the density
factor, e.g. 1 cup flour weighs less than 1 cup butter.
Quantities in ingredients have been rounded up or down for convenience,
where appropriate. Metric conversions may therefore not correspond exactly.
It is important to use either American or metric measurements within a recipe.

© for the original edition: Fabien Bellahsen and Daniel Rouche

Design and production: Fabien Bellahsen and Daniel Rouche
Photographs and technical direction: Didier Bizos
Photographic Assistant: Gersende Petit-Jouvet

Thanks to:
Ministry for Tourism, Leisure and the Craft Industry of Tunisia
National Office of Tunisian Tourism—Tunisia and Paris
National Office of the Tunisian Craft Industry and SOCOPA, Tunisia (Société de Commercialisation des Produits de l'Artisanat)—
Society for the Marketing of Craft Industry Products, Tunisia

Original title: *Tunisie – Délices de Tunisie*
ISBN of the original edition: 2-84690-243-7
ISBN of the German edition: 3-8331-2343-5

© 2006 for the English edition:
Tandem Verlag GmbH
KÖNEMANN is a trademark and an imprint of Tandem Verlag GmbH

Translation from French:
Vivien Groves for Cambridge Publishing Management Limited
Edited by Deborah Campbell-Todd for Cambridge Publishing Management Limited
Proofread by Jan McCann for Cambridge Publishing Management Limited
Typeset and managed by Cambridge Publishing Management Limited

Project Coordinator: Isabel Weiler

Printed in Germany

ISBN 3-8331-2344-3

10 9 8 7 6 5 4 3 2 1
X IX VIII VII VI V IV III II I